The Sanford Meisner Approach

WORKBOOK TWO
emotional freedom

Smith and Kraus *Books For Actors*

CAREER DEVELOPMENT: Technique

CAREER DEVELOPMENT: Actor's Guides

If you require prepublication information about upcoming Smith and Kraus books, you may receive our semiannual catalogue, free of charge, by sending your name and address to *Smith and Kraus Catalogue, P.O. Box 127, Lyme, NH 03768. Or call us at (800) 895-4331, fax (603) 643-1831.*

The Sanford Meisner Approach

WORKBOOK TWO
emotional freedom

Larry Silverberg

Career Development Series

A SMITH AND KRAUS BOOK

Published by Smith and Kraus, Inc.
PO Box 127, Lyme, NH 03768
Copyright ©1997 by Larry Silverberg
Manufactured in the United States of America
Cover and Text Design by Julia Hill

First Edition: May 1997
10 9 8 7 6 5 4 3

The Library of Congress Cataloging-In-Publication Data

Silverberg, Larry, 1959–
     The Sanford Meisner approach: workbook two, emotional freedom /
by Larry Silverberg.

     p. cm. (A career development book)
     ISBN 1-57525-074-8

     1. Acting. 2. Meisner, Sanford. I. Title. II. Series.
     PN2061.S55   1994
     792'.028—dc20   94-38079
                    CIP

acknowledgments

How was I so fortunate to be led to the finest acting teachers of our time. Of course, it's an unanswerable question — so I'll just keep saying "Thank you, God!"

Sandy, I have built a life with the tools you gave to me. Thank you.

Thanks Suzanne for taking the time to write the preface for this book and for your generous feedback. I wanted so much for you to be a part of this book and now you are!

Thanks to Jill, Sarah and Aaron, to Mom and Dad, Debbie, Matthew and Dina, Helen and Skip and my buddy, Dick Kowal — without you, the tank would quickly be on empty.

Thanks Marisa and Eric for your friendship and making me believe that I am an author.

Thanks Julia for making my books look so good!

Thanks to all of my wonderful students in my "Meisner Actors Training Program '97" at my theatre here in Seattle. Remember, *"we're talking about Great Acting!"*

Special thanks Marcie K. Gallagher for taking the time to share with me how important my first Meisner book and this work has been in your life. And thanks to everyone who has written to me with your kind words about the Meisner Book and all my other books. I appreciate your responses to these books more than you know!

For My Daughter,
Sarah

E m o t i o n a l   F r e e d o m

contents

preface

In 1970 I was blessed with the opportunity of studying with Sandy Meisner. The total sense and perfect truth of every stepping stone in those two unforgettable years of classes intoxicated me with a fervor that led me to teach. No one, no one, no one can teach like Sandy. But with a kind of messianic zeal, I presented his exercises as clearly and carefully as I could and, through the many years of teaching, my understanding of the profundity and resonance of his work deepened. But every year, the week before introducing emotional preparation I became anxious, insecure, sleepless and fearful that I might make a mess of it.

I knew the mandate: to present emotional preparation in a way that would entice the actors to make use of the most important ingredients in their personal larder, to whet their appetites to fantasize the fulfillment of their most vital wishes, to acknowledge who and what they most love and to then imagine the best or worst that might befall that love, to summon actors to dream a dream or to suffer a nightmare by inviting an encounter with the deepest and most personal imagery of their lives.

Larry Silverberg's book *Emotional Freedom* would have helped me to feel more confident to introduce this central element of an actor's training. Larry's systematic progression of the exercises and his careful explanations, his thorough evaluation of each actor's work, his clear and gentle guidance of the actors through the taking of an imaginary journey so that they might make a kind of alchemic use of the vital meanings in their lives.

I do not think it is possible to learn to act from reading a book. But, I believe that actors who read Larry Silverberg's book will know the difference between pretending to feel what the "character" feels and actually inhabiting that life with their own. They will also know, on yet another level, the meaning of Sandy's perfect definition: ACTING IS LIVING TRUTHFULLY UNDER IMAGINARY CIRCUMSTANCES. And because of the patient guidance in this book, they will, I hope, want to explore the infinite territory of their imagination.

I congratulate Larry on this book because of its usefulness to actors, to teachers of acting and to directors. It's importance is expressed by Robert Frost:

"Something we were withholding made us weak
until we found it was ourselves."

Thank you, Larry.
Suzanne Shepherd

introduction

The greatest acting teacher of our time, my teacher, Sandy Meisner, died last week. Even though he was so ill this last year and could not teach, it is unimaginable to me that he will no longer be in the classroom. It is unthinkable to me that he will no longer be helping actors arrive at an absolutely uncontrollable and deeply authentic moment, helping actors get out of their own way and igniting their imaginations, helping actors to be more available to both their partners and to their own powerfully creative resources. It is horrifying to me that, like the thousands of actors who were fortunate enough to sit in that classroom with him, thousands more will never have that chance. I miss Sandy so much. I miss the burning arrow he was in my life, always aimed at the heart of the matter, demanding that each and everyone of us be relentless, simple and true.

Out of his passion and his brilliance, Sandy developed a profoundly organic and healthy approach to training actors. Why do I say organic and healthy? Because this work continually invites us to bring our humanness to the stage, our own unique point of view. It is a process that keeps demanding us to shed anything extraneous and false as we fully inhabit the reality of this very moment. It is certainly the most rigorous and the most rewarding work I know. And if you want some examples of the kinds of results that are possible, well, here are just a few of Sandy's students: Robert Duvall, Joanne Woodward, Jon Voight, Gregory Peck, Diane Keaton, Peter Falk, Steve McQueen, Mary Steenburgen, Jeff Goldblum, Tony Randall, Lee Grant and Sydney Pollack.

In case you don't know, Sandy was a founding member of the revolutionary, 1930s New York theatre company, The Group Theatre. This incredible collaborative experiment, which grew out of the most personal vision of theatre great Harold Clurman, is where everything we know as modern American acting sprang from. And when the Group Theatre dissolved in the early 1940s, Sandy Meisner went on to develop and teach his own ways of getting at this thing called "the craft of acting" at the Neighborhood Playhouse School of Theatre in New York City — which is where I studied with him.

This book and the other three I am doing on the Meisner Approach are a simple offering. Sandy gave this work to me and I want to give it to you — very much! As does Sandy's approach, these books work in a step-by-step fashion. Like with a tower of building blocks, the foundation must be laid first and then, it is only the careful placement of each new block that makes the placement of the next block possible. So, if you haven't read my *Meisner Approach: Workbook One* (which is where I lay the foundation,) I suggest you do so — it will make this book vastly more valuable for you. But do feel free to read this book first. If it turns you on, well, go run for the first one.

In the foundation work of *Workbook One*, we worked on strengthening the essential skills of great acting. These abilities include: being led by our instinct rather than our head, living fully in the present, being responsive to our partners in each moment, really doing what we are doing rather than pretending to do what we are doing, being the expression of who we truly are rather than who we think we should be or who others tell us we should be, bringing authentic and personal meaning to everything we do on stage and expanding our actors imagination. Good stuff for actors, don't you think? Not only good, crucial!

And now, I welcome you to *Workbook Two: Emotional Freedom* and I invite you to join me in the next fundamental phase of the Meisner work — "emotional preparation" — as we explore the realm of the emotions and the actors emotional instrument. Ready? Let's go.

Section One
preliminary work

setting the stage

FREEDOM.

Let's take a look:

ease
openness
spontaneity
liberation
unconstrained
unobstructed
unfettered
unimpeded
unconfined

Great words for actors, don't you think?

Continuing from where we left off in *Workbook One,* we are now going to address — very directly — emotion.

That's a big deal for us actors, isn't it. Let's include acting teachers here as well, because this is precisely where many teachers are crippling, even damaging their students, by encouraging various forms of psychological warfare in the classroom. In my experience of working with actors and acting students around the country, the "emotions" are certainly an area of confusion as well as a source of tremendous frustration.

We will be exploring here the part of the Meisner Approach called "emotional preparation." Many people, exposed to only isolated portions of this or that part of the Meisner Approach, have thought that Sandy's use of emotional preparation was simply about getting emotional. Of course, if you take this aspect of the work out of context, that is what it would look like. But it's important to remember that each part of this approach is another building block; we are building something here. And you'll really start to enjoy living in the house when all of the bricks are in place (and like the third little pig, the wise one, let's go the extra mile and build it well.)

What I know is that emotional preparation, in the bigger picture of the actor's craft, is not really about "being emotional" – it is about deepening the actor's availability and connection to what has profound meaning to him or her. And for what purpose? So that we are prepared and ready to take action! So that we know in a very clear and personal way WHY we are taking action! Remember, acting is doing. Acting is not "talking about" and it is not "feeling about," it is doing something. Acting is doing – doing with meaning. We do not go on stage to emote, we go on stage to accomplish something against all odds; we go on stage to fight for what we know is true and right and necessary.

Now in life, what is it do you think that gets us to take action when it is not easy or within our comfort zone to do so? Isn't it always because we have a very strong and personal need? Isn't it always because our feelings about that particular thing run deeply, so deep that we move ourselves past all the head's cautions to wait, to be careful, to do it tomorrow, to leave it alone, that it's not that important anyway, that we're better off where we are, that people may not like us if we follow our impulse to do this thing?

And let's face it, you and I are emotional beings. We are born fully alive emotionally. As infants, we are not only utterly expressive of what's going on with us, we are much more aware of and responsive to the inner state of the people around us — what's actually going on with them — than the words they speak. As adult actors, we must re-open ourselves to that kind of emotional availability because it is true on stage as well, that the words are never really telling the whole story. If the play is to live, we must be aware of and responsive to what's really going on with our partners on stage in each moment.

Also, it is vital that we are able to "realize," to fulfill, the emotional demands of the script. We don't have a violin to play — we are the instrument, and so we want to be able to "play" the full range of our own unique notes; not only the limited range of notes we play in our day-to-day life, the entire range! Now, as we work together, we will be doing some "getting emotional." For a while, you may even become overly "emotion conscious." I find that to be par for the course in this aspect of the work because we are specifically isolating this thing called emotion and putting it under the microscope. Unfortunately, many actors don't then deal with the more advanced and essential aspects of interpretation, and they become trapped in a haze of emotional self-consciousness. (Which is why this is book two of my four book series on the Meisner Approach. Books three and four will be dealing with the acting tools of working with text and interpretation.)

Going back to the violin analogy, if you were a violin student and you worked long and hard enough on the scales, at some point your fingers would go to the notes you want to play without having to think about it. Same thing here. I have found that, out of dealing with emotion directly and discovering ways to work with ourselves in a deeper way, and as we learn specifically where to channel all that we are feeling, we eventually become much less concerned with emotion. And so, ultimately, through this very demanding portion of the Meisner Approach, you will develop a more expansive and richer acting instrument and you will experience greater freedom in your work. Greater freedom. Sounds good, right?

This would be a good time to introduce you to emotional preparation and explain more specifically what it is.

Chapter Two

about emotional preparation

Let's say that you are in a play and you are playing the part of a married gal who is coming home from a bowling tournament. It is the first scene of the play and you have to make your entrance. You are walking into your living room where you discover your husband dusting the furniture. The director has told you that he wants you to do a little celebration dance as you enter. Here are the first three lines of the play:

> Wife (you): Honey, you are looking at a bowler here!
> Husband: Wow, you are on top of the world!
> Wife: We won, babe, we won the tournament big time!

Now, after reading those three lines it is clear and obvious that, as the wife, you are going to be required to make your entrance in an emotionally alive place that will not only make sense of what you say and do when you come in, you must also make it possible for your partner on stage to say his line, *"Wow, you are on top of the world!"* You have got to come into the scene ON TOP OF THE WORLD! Well, how do you go about getting yourself into that kind of triumphant, joyous state while you are off-stage? Remember, in our work, we don't pretend and we don't fake. This means that when you make that entrance, you must not be acting triumphant and joyous — you must actually BE triumphant and joyous.

This is what emotional preparation is all about. It's what you do before you enter so that when you do enter, you are emotionally alive. And as you see from my example, the nature of the preparation you do is dictated by the demands of the play. *"But,"* you say, *"I don't give a damn about bowling or winning a bowling tournament. How am I going to get truly excited about that?"* Great question! You have brought up an amazing and fantastic part of the acting process. Here I am the actor and over there is the playwright's play. It is now my job to take the words given to me by the playwright and invest them with life. You get that? INVEST THEM WITH LIFE! Now there's a juicy statement that turns me on. And invest them with whose life do you think? The character's life? What character? Is the character going to act this part? No, you are. You will invest the words with your life! Now, I get excited when I think about sinking myself into the puzzle, the mystery of creation as an actor. And you know, that's what it's all really about. Do you think all this acting technique stuff is so that you will end up with some sort of "one plus one equals two" kind of formula? Forget about it! All technique is about one thing: making you strong and willing and able to allow the mysterious to occur. Remember, great acting only occurs in the territory of the unknown. Us actors must always return to the land of not knowing because that is the only place it is possible to actually discover anything.

I didn't really answer your question about getting truly excited because of the bowling tournament, when you could care less about bowling. Well, I'm not going to answer that question now. The ways into the very personal solutions for that challenge will be revealed as we work together on the exercises in this book and in my following two books. Let me also note that not every entrance you make in whatever play you are working on will be as heightened emotionally as in the exercises we will be doing together. But in all great plays the stakes are very high and you will be called upon to take on the most extreme circumstances imaginable. So it is vital now, in our exercise work, that you reach further and dig deeper than is comfortable or reasonable to do. As Sandy used to say to us, *"I'm not interested in training actors to bunt, I want to train actors so that they can hit home runs!"*

THE EXERCISES

In our work on emotional preparation, we will begin by doing some new exercises in which you work without a partner. Then we will come back around to the kind of exercises you learned how to do in the first book on this approach using repetition, activities and relationships. As we return to those exercises, we will add new elements, as well as raise the emotional stakes in the way you set up the exercise. You will also see that the activity, which in the previous exercises always had a physical difficulty, takes on a new dimension.

One other thing. Emotional preparation is probably the most elusive part of this whole approach, it is certainly the most personal. What I mean is that, no one can really teach it to you. As we go through the exercises, you will actually begin to discover and develop your own ways of working. I think that's great news, don't you? Listen, as I have said before, I'm not interested in you becoming a great "Meisner actor." What I am interested in is giving you some specific ways to strengthen your own individual craft of acting as you become the most passionately authentic actor you can be. And, as you know, I certainly believe the Meisner Approach is the best way there!

So, let's get to it.

Chapter Three

prelude to emotional preparation

The Sleep Exercise

As a first step into emotional preparation, I want to teach you how to sleep on stage. You may think this an odd place to start. Have you ever thought about what you would do if you had to "sleep" while acting in a play or in a film?

Why wouldn't just closing your eyes and doing things with your breath and face to make it look like you are sleeping be a great choice as an actor?

As we have established, in our approach we do not "make it look like," we do not fake or pretend.

Why also, would actually falling asleep in the scene not be a good choice? (Silly question, right?)

But if you were to really go to sleep, are you available to your partners on stage? Obviously, you are not and you must be in every moment. So how do we "sleep" on stage?

First, we know that acting is doing; that if we are not actively involved in something we are really doing on stage, we are no longer acting. If you recall, I have also taught you that one of the most important keys for an actor is "specificity," that we must be specific in everything we do and that anything left general will result in acting that is general. This means that if we have to be asleep in a scene, as in all of our acting, we must be involved in doing something specific.

THE EXERCISE

You are going to lie down, get comfortable, close your eyes and have a fantasy. I want you to choose the kind of fantasy you will have. What I mean is, pick an emotional direction that you want to fantasize about in this exercise. Whatever direction you pick, it must be in the extreme. For example, you might choose to fantasize about:

- **the most fantastic thing that could ever happen to you**

- **the worst news you could ever receive**

- **the most wonderfully lustful encounter, and so on.**

As you see from the examples, you are not going to choose the details of the fantasy, simply pick an emotional direction you would like the fantasy to go.

Before you give this a try, I want to clarify a few things. What I want you to do in this exercise is to attempt to freely fantasize about whatever emotional direction you have chosen. You see, fantasizing, (we can also call this free associating or daydreaming,) is something we all know how to do — but in our day-to-day lives we either don't take the time to do it fully or when we do begin to get caught up in a daydream, we stay in control of it; we censor it. If it starts to get uncomfortable, we stop it and do something else.

So what I am asking you to do is to have an uncensored fantasy, to let go of controlling it in any way. And hey, why not? The fantasy is your own and you don't have to tell anyone anything about it. It's private. It's just for you. So, I want you to see if you can allow the fantasy to really take you where it is going rather than you taking it where you think it should go or where you would like it to go. Now what if the fantasy starts to veer off from the direction you determined for the exercise? I am telling you to fully allow the fantasy to go where it goes. Don't worry about anything else. If you get out of the way of the fantasy, you will be surprised at where it takes you and how it may come around to the emotional direction you chose in ways you could never have imagined.

That's enough talking for now, I want you to try it. You can do this exercise by yourself or with your acting partner who will serve as the observer. If you work on your own, I want you to set an alarm clock to "wake you up" from the fantasy in about ten minutes. If you are working with a partner, or in a group, I want the observer to simply stop you in about ten minutes. (Of course, if you are working in a group, each person should do each step I talk about before you all return and continue in the book.)

Do the "sleep" exercise now. Then read on.

. . .

Please respond to this question in the following space: What was your experience in fantasizing? I am not asking you to write about the fantasy itself, I am asking you to write some notes about what it was like to try to have a free and uncensored fantasy. What was it like to try and really allow the fantasy to take you rather than you leading it?

_____

_____

_____

_____

_____

_____

_____

_____

_____

_____

_____

_____

_____

Before continuing with the book, I want you to do the sleep exercise one more time, with one change — pick a different emotional direction for the fantasy this time; go in a different direction than you went in the first exercise. So go ahead and do that now.

. . .

How did that go for you? Please don't expect any huge results from yourself right now, I simply wanted you to have the experience of starting to allow yourself to fantasize without inhibitions; of seeing where your imagination will take you when you try to give it full reign. So, not only have we begun our journey into emotional preparation, now you know how to sleep on stage. When the fantasy you have chosen really takes root in you, it will produce its own physical and emotional life and you would appear to the audience to be sleeping and dreaming. And depending on the scene in the play (or film) you would choose to have the kind of fantasy that would lead you to the specific kind of sleep you would need to be having — is the character having guilt ridden nightmares or is she dreaming about a great political victory? Also, when you get fully involved in your fantasy, if you have to either wake up on your own or be woken up by someone else in the scene, you would be emerging from a very specific place and it would appear to the audience that you are truly coming out of a deep sleep state. By the way, doesn't this way of sleeping on stage sound alot more personally engaging and alot more fun than just pretending to sleep? It is!

getting ready

As we begin the series of emotional preparation exercises, I want to mention a few things.

In the first two exercises I am about to give you, in which you will be working by yourself, I do want you to have at least one other person with you who will serve as the observer. As we get into the exercises where we reintroduce the partner, I want you to work in a group of three so that two people will do the exercise and the third person will be the observer. The main thing I ask the observer to do is to tell the person or people working when to stop the exercise. In that way, you don't have to worry about when you should stop the exercise on your own. Also, as in a class, the fact that there is someone else there witnessing what you are doing in the exercise adds an important ingredient to the work itself.

With each exercise, I will first give you the setup and then, any instructions for that exercise. After you read those directions:

1. I want you to take at least a day to set up and get yourself ready to do the exercise.

2. When you are ready, do the exercise.

3. I will then give you one blank page in the book to do your journal work. Please do the journal work immediately after you have actually done the exercise — notes about your experience, impressions, how you set up the elements for that exercise, questions you might have about the exercise, and so forth.

4. After that, please continue to read the book. As I did in *Workbook One*, I will be giving you my invented interactions with invented students who have just completed an invented exercise. (Oh Boy! I get to do a lot of inventing here. That's my favorite part!)

5. Then, I want you to do that level of the exercise one more time. So take at least another day to set up a new exercise.

6. When ready, come back and do the exercise.

7. As before, take some time to write your journal notes after this exercise. There will be blank pages in the book for these notes.

So, you see that you will be doing the exercise and the journal work two times for each of the exercises. After you have completed all of that, you may move on to the next session in the book.

Section Two
emotional preparation
THE EXERCISES

coming home to be alone

Setup

In this exercise you have just found out something or something has just happened that is extremely meaningful to you.

Out of this event or this new information, you come home to be alone.

Instructions

Since this is the first exercise, I want to go over a few things specifically before you get started. First, let's talk about the thing you are going to create to work from — what it is that you have just found out or what has just happened, out of which you are coming home to be alone. As you learned how to do in *Workbook One,* this circumstance must be invented out of your imagination and based on an element of truth. That element of truth is its importance to you. Remember? To be very clear, I want to review together this essential aspect of our working together.

Let's say that in your life right now, you have recently found out that your husband or your wife wants a divorce and you are devastated and shattered. Then, to do this emotional preparation exercise, you choose to come home to be alone after finding out that your husband or your wife wants a divorce. It certainly gets you into an emotionally alive place — but why is this not a good choice of a circumstance to work from?

Although this circumstance is extremely meaningful to you, where is the element of imagination here? Imaginary! The circumstance you create must be an imaginary circumstance based on an element of truth. Again, if we are talking about emotional freedom, this is certainly one of the primary keys. Why?

First of all, our actual experiences are limited. We've each had only so many deeply meaningful events in our lives. Are you going to use the death of your puppy when you were ten every time you have to be sad in a play? What happens when, after one hundred performances of the play, the emotional impact of that actual event is not as potent. If all we know how to do is use actual past events, we are restricted in our ability to work.

But our imagination is infinite!

Our imagination is also more persuasive. Why, do you think? I believe, basically, because using our actors imagination is a more healthy tool to work with. Let's take the divorce example from above. If you are really in the middle of that in your life and you are using it to get upset for your entrance in the play, do you think your insides really want to go through that intense pain every night you do the play – when you are already living with it in your every waking moment? Do you think that's a good and healthy thing for you as a human being? No, I don't think so.

Or, say you are using the death, seven years ago, of your grandmother to get into a certain emotional state for your entrance into a scene in the play. Again, something in us, obviously, doesn't really want to re-experience the pain of that event again and again and again. But with our imagination, we can freely create any circumstance – because when it is over, it's over. Do you understand? If I have to be in a rage as I make my entrance into the play, all I have to do is imagine some deranged creep hurting my daughter or my son and I'm ready to go. Now, my insides can accept and embrace that imaginary circumstance fully because first, the element of truth has great meaning to me – in this case, it is everything that my daughter and my son mean to me – and second, because the rest of the circumstance is invented, it is easier for me to take it on "as if" it were true. Then, when the play is over, I know that my children are fine and that I can go home and give them big hugs. Now, isn't that clearly a healthier way of working?

I should also point out here, that to work with a circumstance that is completely imaginary is not sufficient. Suppose you invented a situation in which you were deeply jealous of your sister because she has just had her life's dream come true and you are still struggling — but the truth is you don't even have a sister. Well, how can this really mean anything to you? "But" you say, "I have friends that I would be jealous of if they were to suddenly achieve great success." Great! Then create the circumstance based on the specific friend whose success would have that impact on you. You see, the circumstance must be imaginary and it must always be based on an element of truth. Again, the element of truth is its true importance to you! Without the element of truth, there is no way for that imaginary circumstance to take root in you.

One more unnatural thing about the use of actual events from our past is that how we once responded to past events doesn't really represent who we are today. So, not only is the use of actual events in our past a limiting and unhealthy way of working, it is not an organic way of working with what has deep meaning to us today. I believe where the really vital aspects of each one of us lives, is in what is of great meaning to us RIGHT NOW! Look, in every element, theatre is an art of "right now" not "back then." I want you to hear that again. In every element theatre is an art of "right now" not "back then."

This brings up one last element I want to mention in your setting up the circumstances. Whether you create something to work from that has just happened or from something that you have just found out, the key here is in the word JUST. It did not happen last week and you didn't find it out yesterday. It is crucial that it has JUST HAPPENED or you have JUST FOUND IT OUT. And then you come home to be alone.

So, again, here is the setup for the first exercise:

In this exercise you have just found out something or something has just happened that is extremely meaningful to you.

Out of this event or this new information, you come home to be alone.

After you have taken at least a day to create the specific and imaginary circumstance you will be working with, you will do the exercise. To do the exercise, you will go out and do an emotional preparation based on that circumstance. This means that you will go out and have an uncensored fantasy about that thing which you have decided has just happened or you have just found out. When you feel that your fantasy is working on you, you will come home to your room to be alone. Once you come in, simply see what happens. The exercise ends when the observer tells you it is over.

Go ahead now and set up your exercise. After you have done the exercise, take some time to write your journal notes here in the book. Then continue reading the book.

_____

_____

_____

_____

_____

_____

_____

Example Exercise: Brenda

Larry: Let's talk about the exercise Brenda. First, I want you and the whole class to know something important about this work on emotional preparation and how I will be working with you. Listen, your fantasy life is your business and I will never ask you to talk about the details of your preparations. I will ask you how you set up the imaginary circumstances that you are working with so we can talk about how to fine tune it or adjust it if it didn't take you very far – or – when it does work well for you, I'll ask you to share the setup so that the class gets good examples of working with powerful circumstances. Also, as I have done in our previous exercises *(Workbook One)* when the circumstance doesn't work for you, if you wish to, I will explore the circumstance with you to see if and how you could make it more specifically meaningful. I will also ask what your experience of doing the emotional preparation was so that you can define for yourself what is and isn't working in the actual process of trying to prepare. If you want to share anything about the details of the fantasy, you are free to do so, but it is very important to me that you understand that you are never required to do so. In fact, as we are talking about the exercise, in every moment and at all times, you have every right to say, "I don't want to talk about that," or, "It's none of your business." Is that clear?

Brenda: Yes, thanks for telling me that. That really gives me the feeling that I am in charge here.

Larry: Yes, you are.

Brenda: Also, it makes me feel safer to go fully into my fantasy knowing that I don't have to tell everyone everything about what I was imagining. I was worried about that.

Larry: Good. So, let's talk about your exercise. Before I ask how you set up the circumstance, I want you to tell me about your experience of going out of the room and preparing.

Brenda: Well, first of all, I'm really feeling like a failure. I don't know, no matter what I tried I just couldn't seem to get into it; get into the thing I set up to prepare from. I... hmmm. I don't know...

Larry: Now look. Is this a new exercise for you?

Brenda: Yes.

Larry: Did you try to do it?

Brenda: Yes.

Larry: Then please, come on now, get off of your own back. Isn't it enough that too many other people are ready to criticize us? And, you simply must come to this work with the humility of a student, as well as with a respect for the works difficulty. You must stay close to the fact that you are here to learn and that every experience will take you one step closer to where you want to go. So, are you a failure Brenda?

Brenda: *(laughing)* I am not a failure, I just learned something. But I don't know what I learned.

Larry: Okay, let's talk about it. Now when you went...

Brenda: Larry, I did want to say something else about what I just said.

Larry: What's that?

Brenda: Well, in our exercises with activities and partners (Brenda is talking about the exercises I teach in *Workbook One.*) we did have to go out of the room and think about our circumstance that brought us to the room. So, it's not like this is totally a new thing. I guess that is why I thought I should have done better than I did — but I just kept getting stuck.

Larry: You're right, this isn't a totally new thing in that everything we have done in the foundation exercises have been leading to the point where we now must deal specifically with what you do when you go out of the room and get ready to come in. You see, before, I purposely left what you did outside of the room totally general. All I told you was to go out and think about your circumstance and when you were ready, to come and knock. Although we were certainly interested in the meaning you were able to bring to the door when you were the person outside the room, our emphasis was much more on what happened when you came into the room and worked with your partner. Right now, we are shifting the focus primarily to what you do when you are outside of the room. This, and the fact that you are coming home to be alone, with no partner to work off of when you get into the room, puts new demands on you. So, these elements, make it a very new exercise, you see?

Brenda: Yes, I understand.

Larry: So, you say that you kept getting stuck. Tell me about that.

Brenda: Well, maybe stuck isn't the word. I was getting distracted.

Larry: In what ways?

Brenda: Well, there were two people talking out in the hall and it was hard for me to think about my circumstance. They distracted me for a while and then they left and I found that I would look around and I got distracted by seeing the pictures on the walls as well as all the activity I could see outside on the street through the window... Things like that.

Larry: When you go out to do the emotional preparation, and this is for all of you, I suggest you go find a little dark nook where you can really be by yourself and where you don't have those kinds of distractions.

Brenda: But what about when you are working on a film set and you don't have a place like that to go and you've got all these people around you talking and hanging lights and all that?

Larry: Right now, I think you really need to have a private little space to prepare in. As you strengthen in your ability to work with yourself in this way, you will become more flexible and adaptable to whatever situation you find yourself in. You will see that what are now distractions, ultimately, can be funneled directly into whatever preparation you are involved in. You see, as you are fantasizing, if things around you come into your awareness, rather than trying to block them out of your mind so that you can get back to your fantasy — see what happens if you allow those very things to take the fantasy to where it goes next. Do you understand?

Brenda: I'm not sure...

Larry: I'll give you an example. Suppose my circumstance was that I just found out that my best friend, who had gone to a war-torn foreign country as a medical volunteer, was killed when his truck ran over a land mine. Now suppose that, as I am fantasizing, there is a car outside that starts blasting its horn. Well I could get angry about the distraction and permit it to stop my fantasy — or — if I allow it to, I might find that the cars horn takes me deeper into the fantasy. I suddenly find myself imagining the driver of another truck who sees both the land mine and my friends truck approaching it. He starts blowing his horn and screaming as he tries to keep my friend's truck from getting blown up. Then the horn outside stops and I find myself imagining the driver who has seen the land mine jumping out of his truck and running to try and get my friend's truck to stop but the driver of my friend's truck is looking in another direction and he hits the land mine with the front left tire. I see the driver who tried to stop them watch in horror as the blast sends the entire truck twenty feet into the air on fire.

Brenda: So you are saying that it is better to embrace whatever things come into my mind rather than try to block them out because they don't fit into what I think I'm supposed to be thinking about.

Larry: Exactly! That's a very important word, embrace. You must embrace exactly what is going on. Remember, we are talking about an uncensored, uninhibited fantasy in which you are letting it take you where it is going rather than you taking it where you think it should go.

Brenda: Well, I clearly wasn't doing that. I let every distraction get in my way and each time I was distracted, I tried to get my mind back on track.

Larry: That's a great awareness. And remember, there is no track. But if we were to use a track analogy, it would be more like you are discovering the path of the track as you are actually laying each section of the track down.

Brenda: I see that now.

Larry: So, after all of these distractions, what did you do?

Brenda: I gave up and came into the room.

Larry: Okay, so you tried to prepare, you got distracted and then you gave up and came in.

Brenda: Yes.

Larry: Good. So, next time, don't give up. And as I said, go find some dark little corner somewhere to prepare in.

Brenda: All right.

Larry: I don't want to discuss how you set up the circumstance because you never got to explore it. You can try to use it again or choose something new, it's up to you.

. . .

Example Exercise: Blake

Larry: Blake, tell me what the imaginary circumstances were that you prepared from, how did you set it all up?

Blake: Well, I... what I decided was that I just got a call from Sydney Pollack and he said that he had a part for me in a new film he is making with Robert Redford.

Larry: Here's what I saw happen. When you came in, you were somewhat pleased. That state of pleasure passed very quickly and you sat down and tried to figure out what you should do next.

Blake: But I was excited to find out I got the part.

Larry: Really? It wasn't in your behavior.

Blake: But I'm telling you I was excited.

Larry: Now look, getting to work with Sydney Pollack and Robert Redford may actually mean a lot to you, but it certainly wasn't living in you yet. If getting that part is the most incredible and wonderful break in your life, then I'd think you'd come home in the midst of the biggest celebration imaginable. That wasn't happening. What was happening was that you were somewhat pleased. There's a big difference between "somewhat pleased" and "the biggest celebration of my life!" You tell me, do you actually think you came home in the midst of the biggest celebration of your life?

Blake: Well, no, I guess I wasn't in that kind of place, no...

Larry: That's what we are shooting for here. You see? A full preparation! So that when you come in, it isn't possible for you to sit down and figure out what to do next because you are too involved in DOING IT — whatever that "doing it" is. I'm not telling you what you should be doing when you come in and I am not telling you what your celebration should look like. I'm certainly not saying that you have to be jumping up and down — who knows what form your own celebration of this event would take. I am telling you that if working with Pollack and Redford is that meaningful to you and you took that on for all it's worth, if you really "accepted" that imaginary circumstance, the impact of this event would take you on a ride that would be totally out of your control.

Blake: Larry, is it okay if I talk about the meaning of all this to me for a moment?

Larry: Of course.

Blake: The truth is, I want desperately to work with Sydney Pollack. And, I don't know, it's not just about being in a movie or even about getting ahead in my career. And although a bigger income would be nice, it's certainly not about the money! Part of it is that Sydney is such an actor's director, he really understands the actors process, which so few directors really know anything about —

and I want so much to learn from him. Also, I have had some success in other areas of my life and I have this deep thing going on in me — it's about... well, I feel I have so much to offer and I want to reach more people than I have ever reached before. I just want to work on a film that is meaningful in some way and act in a part that I can make a difference in people's lives in some way. I know that's not something that you can really plan for, but... I want to have that chance badly — to reach more people. You know? To reach more people. God, I actually even got Sydney Pollack on the telephone in his office in Los Angeles. I actually got him on the phone, and I could hardly talk! I don't know what the hell he must've thought of me. Somehow, after sounding like a total idiot, I finally came around to the fact that I wanted to send him my picture and resume. I asked if he would please consider me if he was working on a film that had something in it that I could audition for. Here I am sitting and talking to Sydney Pollack, fumbling like a fool on my words and sweat pouring down my body!

Larry: How did he respond?

Blake: He simply said, "Sure, send me the picture and resume." I know it's a long shot, I mean why would he really bother to bring me all the way in to LA to audition...

Larry: Hey, at least you made the call, you made the attempt. You know, most people never do. That takes some chutzpah. *(That's yiddish for "balls.")* And what will come of sending your picture, you just never know! I hope your dream comes true. Getting back to the exercise, we now know that your circumstance is very meaningful to you but that the preparation didn't take you very far. So, let's examine that part of it. I'll say something here. I noticed that you went out to prepare and then you "came home to be alone" very quickly. Talk about that.

Blake: Well, I went out and found a quiet place to prepare. I started to fantasize about the circumstance and as I imagined hearing Sydney Pollack on the phone with me, telling me that he had a part for me, I got real happy and ran to get back home; to get back into the room.

Larry: So you had a sudden rush of emotion and you tried to get back in real fast while it was still going on in you.

Blake: Yeah, that's right.

Larry: Very often, when students first start to do emotional preparations, they come in before they are really prepared. That's what just happened with you. You got a rush of emotion and so you wanted to get in the room and do "the exercise" while you were still in that state. What I suggest is that when you experience that first "rush," don't come in! Stay in the fantasy and allow that rush to take you where it is going. You may even seem to totally "lose it" and get scared that the feeling won't come back at all. But, if you remain relaxed and open, the fantasy will lead you to places you never could have imagined, and those initial feelings will deepen and will become even more persuasive. This simply takes patience and trusting yourself.

Blake: Something you just said really rang true for me. I did get scared that if I didn't come in as soon as I felt that sense of excitement, that I would have nothing going on when I came into the room. But looking back at it now, what I really found out was that in hurrying back into the room, I quickly lost the connection to my circumstance and I found myself in the room with nothing to do. Also, I guess if I am worried about getting into the room so that I can do a "good" exercise, that means that I am not really all that involved with my imaginary circumstance to begin with.

Larry: Those are great lessons for today. So what will you do next time?

Blake: Well, I know what I won't do. I won't zoom back to the room when I have a first rush of some feeling about my imaginary circumstance. And what I will do is take more time to see where the fantasy leads me next; so I can get more personally connected with the event I am fantasizing about.

Larry: Good. You take the time you need to fully prepare. Right?

Blake: Right.

Session One, Exercise Two

Please take at least a day to set up another exercise. After you have done the exercise, use the following page to do your journal work. When you have completed that, move on to the next session.

coming home to do

Setup

> In this exercise you have just found out some-
> thing, or something has just happened that is
> extremely meaningful to you.
>
> Out of this event or this new information, you
> come home to do something.

Instructions

As you can see, we have taken the first exercise and added one element to it. Now, when you come home, you are coming home to do something. What do you think it is that determines how you choose what you will be coming home to do? Here's an example of a circumstance. Read the circumstance and then, on the blank lines, tell me three things that you might then come home to do:

Last week the doctors discovered that _____ needs to have a bone-marrow transplant to live. (Fill in the blanks with the person you are closest to in the whole world.) You have just come from a meeting with _____, and with the doctors, at which the doctors informed you that there is a stranger in another country who has been determined to be a good match for the transplant and who has offered to do the transplant to save _____'s life.

Having just received this most wonderful news, you are now coming home to...

1. _____

2. _____

3. _____

As you now see, what you come home "to do" is a direct result of what has just happened or what you have just found out. The specific thing you invent and choose to do, comes from the circumstance you set up and how that circumstance incites your actor's imagination. The circumstance creates in you A POWERFUL NEED and the thing you come home to do is in response to that need. Do you see that?

Let's say that in the example above, I filled in the blanks with my *wife* and lets's say that out of that circumstance, I am coming home to write a thank-you letter to the stranger who is going to give my wife the chance to live by donating her bone marrow. I am writing the letter because I have a deep need to express to this person how greatful I am.

Or, to try and keep my wife's spirits up so that the operation will go the best it possibly can, I could be coming home to wrap and pack everything that is special to my wife so that she can have them all around her in her foreign hospital room.

If you read the previous book, you can certainly relate what you are now coming home to do, to "the activity." But there is a difference. The activity that you learned how to do in *Workbook One* always had to be extremely physically difficult. Now it doesn't. Obviously, the activity must be extremely meaningful but the difficulty need no longer be a physical one. The difficulty of this new activity, or the challenge of it, is really an emotional one. Here's a powerful example of this kind of "coming home to do" from an exercise a woman did in class a few years ago. (I have to tell you, as the father of two children, a seven-year-old daughter and a three-year-old son, this is one that is hard for me to even write about.)

> **The setup of the circumstances was that the woman had just found out that her young daughter had died. She then came home to pick out an outfit for her daughter to wear in the coffin.**

This is a great example of how the activity that this woman chose to come home to do was not physically difficult, but it was one that had a tremendous emotional difficulty. You also see that the thing she chose to come home to do was in direct relation to the setup of the circumstances and her deep need to respond to those circumstances. Is that clear?

As with all activities, be sure that whatever it is that you come home to do, you bring everything you need to accomplish it. Depending on how you set up the exercise, you may put all the things in the room before you go out to do your emotional preparation, or you may bring them "back home" with you when you come in — whatever makes sense in your own setup. In the example I just gave you, the student brought in lots of her daughter's clothes and she put them in the room so that when she "came home" she could look through them to choose an outfit. Going back to the first example, if I was going to write a letter to the stranger who was going to save my wife's life, I might "bring home" with me a beautiful card that I had "just purchased at a store" to write the thank you letter on.

So, there it is. You will go out and do a full preparation based on the circumstances that you set up and, when you are prepared, you come home to do the thing you have chosen to do. Do not try and figure out or plan how you will do the thing you are coming home to do. That, leave alone. You will discover how to do it when you are actually trying to do it. Here again is the setup:

> **In this exercise you have just found out something, or something has just happened that is extremely meaningful to you.**
>
> **Out of this event or this new information, you come home to do something.**

As a reminder, here is what I want you to do now. (This is the last time I will repeat these steps.)

1. I want you to take at least a day to set up and get yourself ready to do the exercise.

2. When you are ready, do the exercise.

3. I will then give you one blank page in the book to do your journal work. Please do the journal work immediately after you have actually done the exercise.

4. After that, please continue to read the book.

5. Then, I want you to do this level of the exercise one more time. So take at least another day to set up a new exercise.

6. When ready, come back and do the exercise.

7. As before, take some time to write your journal notes after this exercise.

Remember, you will be doing the exercise and the journal work two times for each of the exercises. After you have completed all of that, you may move on to the next exercise in the book.

Go ahead now and set up your exercise. After you have done the exercise, take some time to write your journal notes here in the book. Then continue reading.

Example Exercise: Jane

(Jane is sitting on the sofa and sewing. She's working on a pair of very small denim pants which are torn. She has tried a few times to cut one of the legs of the pants with scissors but, with each attempt, she began sobbing and couldn't do it. She's crying right now as she puts down the needle and she cannot find a tissue to blow her nose in.)

Larry: Okay Jane, let's stop here. *(Joy brings a tissue up to Jane.)* Thanks Joy. Jane, I want you to take your time and tell us what the basic set up of your circumstances were and what you came home to do.

Jane: All right... *(Jane remains quiet and looks down at the floor. Suddenly, she grabs a pillow from the couch, closes her eyes and cries.)* I can't, Oh God, I can't.

Larry: Jane.

Jane: *(Jane cries, her eyes remain closed.)*

Larry: Jane, would you look at me? *(After a few moments, Jane opens her eyes and looks at Larry. Her crying has subsided.)* Jane, I want you to tell me who the exercise was about.

Jane: My youngest brother Todd.

Larry: Where is Todd right now?

Jane: Uh... he's in school, he's in second grade. Mmm... What time is it right now?

Larry: You know, I lost my watch again. *(looks at the class)* Who has the time?

Aaron: It's almost noon.

Jane: He's probably eating his lunch right now.

Larry: Do you know what he's having for lunch today?

Jane: Well, he has to have five things in his lunch box — apple juice in the little box with the straw on it, string cheese, barbecue potato chips, these little packets called "Cheez'n Breadsticks," and for his treat *(She starts laughing.)* he has to have eight of those little orange candy corns that you get at Halloween.

Larry: Not seven candy corns?

Jane: No, it has to be eight!

Larry: I like him, he's very specific!

Jane: Very! I pack his lunch with him in the mornings. I keep suggesting other options but he won't eat anything else. In first grade, his best friend Oliver had to have peanut butter and jelly sandwiches everyday. So Todd ate peanut butter and jelly all year. But, this year, Oliver decided that he would no longer bring sandwiches to school. So, of course, Todd won't either. They have to have the same food as each other and they have to eat the same thing every day.

Larry: So you know that Todd is okay.

Jane: Yes, he's fine.

Larry: Good. I'd like you to tell us the imaginary circumstance you set up and from which you did an emotional preparation.

Jane: Well..., this is so hard to say out loud. I set up that I was rushing off to an audition and that I didn't see Todd behind the car on the driveway as I was backing up the car and *(Tears run down Jane's face but this time she talks through the tears.)* I.... Well, I ran over one of his legs. I just came from the hospital where I found out that they had to amputate the leg.

Larry: *(turns to the class)* Now look, when you set up a powerful circumstance and then, when you really take it on as Jane did here, it's going to stay with you for a while. It's impossible just to drop it as if it never occurred. Now, the more we work in this manner, we become, well, it's like we become a bigger container which can hold all that we feel. And each one of us must find our own way of dealing with the impact on us from the meanings we are taking on — there's no one right way. Whether it's sitting down and writing about it, going out and running, being with a close friend or being alone and meditating, we all have to find our own ways of "coming down from" these heightened realities we are living out so that we can replenish ourselves. *(Larry turns back to Jane.)* Jane, now tell us what you came home to do.

Jane: In the accident, his pants got ripped. They are his favorite pants and I want to fix them for him to put on when he's well enough to get dressed. I also had the scissors because, because I wanted to... *(Jane cannot speak and she is biting her lower lip.)*

Larry: That's all right Jane, you don't need to say any more. *(to the class)* I want you all to notice that Jane put everything she needed to do the activity in the room before she went out to prepare – except for the pants. She had the pants with her when she came into the room, which was justified by the setup of her exercise. Also, though it was so painful to do and, at times, Jane could hardly look at the pants or even hold them, she kept returning to her attempt to complete her work on the pants. To fix them was so personally important to her.

Jane: I want to say something about having the pants with me when I was preparing Larry. Having them with me, really made a difference in doing the emotional preparation. I didn't plan it that way, but when I was out there preparing, I had the pants in my hands and just looking at them and being able to touch them really did something to me. It really swept me away.

Larry: What you are saying is that having the pants with you helped you to more fully accept the imaginary circumstance.

Jane: Yes, it did.

Larry: Great! That's a wonderful discovery and one that will open up many possibilities for your preparations. Remember, this whole thing of emotionally preparing is a very personal process and ultimately, we will all find our own ways to do it. We are talking about strengthening your actor's faith, right? Your ability to accept the imaginary circumstances and live them out as if they were true.

Listen Jane, that was very powerful work and your courage to go to a place that was so extremely meaningful for you and your willingness to explore something uncomfortable to even imagine, had a huge payoff. A payoff in terms of your own aliveness and in terms of authentic human behavior. Remember, that's our job as actors, to bring truthful human behavior to the stage.

Session Two, Exercise Two

Please take at least a day to set up another exercise. After you have done the exercise, use the following space to do your journal work. When you have completed that, move on to the next session.

_____

_____

_____

_____

_____

_____

_____

_____

_____

roommates

Setup

One partner goes out to do an emotional preparation based on something that has just happened or that he or she has just found out — which is extremely meaningful. When you are fully prepared, you come home.

The other partner is in the room.

The relationship is roommates.

Instructions

As you see, we are now reintroducing the partner into the exercise. This means that you will be using repetition, as you learned how to do in *Workbook One,* as the vehicle to work off of each other. For the observer, this is a good time to make sure the partners are not slipping into automatic or robotlike repeating. They must be freely and instinctively working off of each other from their own points of view. (Please review the first book if you have any questions.)

Also, the relationship is roommates. This means that you both live in this room and so, the person coming home need not knock on the door. You go out, prepare and, when you are ready, you come home. Do you know that you are coming home to your roommate? No, all you know is that this extremely meaningful thing has just occurred and that you are coming home. In this exercise, you are not coming home "to do" something, you are only coming home.

For the person in the room, what are you doing there? Are you waiting to have an exercise with your partner? No, you are simply in your room. If your roommate should come home, your job is to "be with" him or her. This means, you must work off of him or her; work off what is happening with your partner and what that does to you. Remember, don't do anything unless something makes you do it and, as you have learned, the something that makes you do what you do is in 1) what is happening with your partner and 2) the impact that has on you.

Go ahead and set up your exercise. After you have done the exercise and written your journal notes, read on.

Example Exercise: Tom and Steve

Larry: Tom, what was the set up of your circumstance from which you prepared.

Tom: I set up that I just got a call from my girlfriend. She told me that she's not going to go on this big weekend skiing trip with me that we had planned.

Larry: And how do you feel about that?

Tom: I'm pissed off.

Larry: Really?

Tom: Well, yeah, she's ruined my weekend.

Larry: So what?

Tom: What do you mean so what?

Larry: I'm asking you, so what, you're weekend's ruined.

Tom: Hey, it really sucks.

Larry: Listen Tom, all that indication, all that jumping around and banging the furniture didn't mean anything. It was a lie and we all knew it. So your weekend was ruined, who cares?

Tom: Hey, I don't appreciate getting fucked over by her, man.

Larry: Now look, Tom, I'm going to tell you something. In all this time of working with you, I still don't know what has real meaning to you. In each exercise, you have avoided grappling with the essential nugget of this work which is the imaginary circumstance based on an element of truth – in other words – we must take the time and make the effort to build an exercise based on something which has a deep and true impact on us. I have been very patient with you and I have tried to make this very clear but I really have to ask you at this point Tom, why are you still here?

Tom: I thought we were supposed to talk about the exercise.

Larry: That's exactly my point. Now, you've made some progress in the time you have been here and at the same time, it has been obvious that, at every turn, you have done the least amount of work possible to get by. And, you continue to hang on for dear life to all that theatrical garbage that you were doing in the beginning of the year. You still want to come in here and impress us with your own notion of "great acting" and you still do the very least amount of work possible. And if you remember, you came to this class talking about how this was the most important thing in the world to you. I'll tell you something, words are very cheap, they are very easy. To tell you the truth, right now, I'm really tired of working with you Tom and I don't know if we can continue.

Tom: *(after a very long silence)* I...I, uh...I don't know what to say.

Larry: I want you to go take a long walk around the block, Tom, and I ask that you really figure out what it is that you want. If you want to continure here, I will demand that you immediately begin to put in some extraordinary effort; I will demand that every time you come to class, you are absolutely prepared to work. I really don't care about the results, I am interested in the effort, in the true caring and importance you place on this work. Go ahead, please take all of your things with you. And if you want to come back and say anything to me, please do so. Whichever way you want to go with this, I want a decision from you today.

Tom: All right. *(Tom goes to his seat and picks up his planner book and puts it in his backpack. The class is very quiet. Tom puts his jacket on and leaves.)*

Larry: Sorry about that Steve. Anyway, your work was fine. You worked off of him very appropriately. From your point of view, he was being a jerk and acting like a clown and you let him know it. We'll get you with a new partner so you can work again next time.

Steve: Okay, thanks.

Example Exercise: Garry and Louise

Larry: Okay Garry, okay let's stop there.

Garry: *(Garry is still walking on his tippy-toes around the room, his fists raised in the air. He's laughing and crying at the same time.)* YES! YES! YES! YES! LET'S STOP THERE! LET'S STOP THERE! *(Larry and the class all laugh. Garry grabs a chair, twirls it around and sits on it, he's out of breath.)*

Larry: *(Larry yells out.)* Garry my friend, what's the great news!

Garry: *(Garry leaps back to his feet and throws his fists back into the air. He yells back:)* I'M HAVING A BABY!! *(Everyone laughs again and Mathew screams out "CONGRATULATIONS!" More laughter from the class.)*

Larry: Okay, okay, good. Wonderful work Garry. A real breakthrough in your work today, yes?

Garry: *(Garry can't stop smiling.)* Wow, yes, yes.

Larry: And you see the impact you had on all of us.

Garry: Oh gee, this is great. I'm not sure what all just happened. Can we talk about it?

Larry: Yes, let's talk about it. First of all, up until now, you have been having some difficulty really accepting the imaginary circumstances that you were setting up, right?

Garry: Yea, I sure was.

Larry: The depth which you took on the imaginary circumstances as if they were true, today, was very new for you. How do you think this came about.

Garry: Well...

Larry: You know, first, let me ask you to tell us how you set up the circumstance from which you prepared.

Garry: I came from having coffee with my girlfriend of three years at our favorite cafe. She just told me that she is pregnant with our child. Wow!

Larry: That's great. Now, what about my other question, about the explosion into this new kind of work today.

Garry: Explosion is a good word for it. I have been so frustrated and upset the past few weeks because I felt that I just wasn't getting this emotional preparation stuff at all. I was getting so tight in my head about it, I thought I was going to explode. Anyway, I knew I wanted to go in a positive and joyful direction with my circumstances this time. The past four times, I had tried creating circumstances that were awful or enraging and basically, I was sick of thinking about that kind of stuff. But I was so frustrated and I was determined to figure out what the hell would make me feel really good about life right now. I remembered a word you used in class last time – obsessed – you said that we really need to become obsessed in our aim at putting together the elements of the exercise. Which, right now means, the extreme meaning we are working with. And I did. I became obsessed with putting the exercise together and I kept thinking about it at work, I thought about it while I was eating, I thought about it when I was going to bed... And when I decided on this circumstance about having a baby, I became obsessed in my thoughts about that and how much it would mean to me right now. When I was walking on the street, I paid special attention to people with babies and kids and that really did something to me. I did another thing yesterday that was really special for me.

Larry: What was that?

Garry: I went to an infant's clothing store and just spent an hour looking at clothes as if I was shopping for my new baby. That was an incredible thing for me.

Larry: Let me tell you something Garry, That's absolutely fantastic! This is working like an actor. And, as we've talked about before, your going the extra mile in terms of your own creativity will always have big dividends.

Garry: I also wanted to say something I discovered while I was out there doing my emotional preparation. Can I talk about that?

Larry: Of course.

Garry: Well, when I tried to prepare before, I always got kind of lost in these very big stories about what I was preparing about. Today, I don't know exactly how it happened, but my mind landed on a baby's hand and I saw — oh God, I can't believe how powerful this is for me — in my mind, I just kept looking at the baby's hand wrapped around my finger, this tiny little chubby hand wrapped around my finger... *(Garry starts to cry.)* I don't know, I just kept looking at that image and I didn't think about anything else, it was so amazing, so powerful, and then I came into the room.

Larry: Thanks for sharing that with us Garry. That's a great discovery. It reminds me of a quote I heard which went something like "Life is found in the details." What you found out, once again, brings us back to something I said to all of you very early on and that is that "the way in" for us actors is through specificity. Remember that? This is a wonderful lesson for all of us in terms of the emotional preparation. Yes, Erica, did you want to ask something?

Erica: It's not really a question. Ummm, this may sound kind of weird, but, there was a moment in the exercise when Garry was sitting on the floor and he just looked down at his hand and you know how you can have a whole little fantasy in about three seconds? Well, when Garry looked down at his hand, this is so amazing to me, he just glanced down at his hand while he was sitting there on the floor and I had this whole little fantasy of him sitting there with an infant on a blanket and the infant holding on tightly to Garry's finger. I mean that is so weird!

Larry: You know, it's not weird, it's the result of Garry being that specific and that authentically involved. Isn't that great? And that's the kind of gift we give to the audience when we pay the price and bring such a personal and rich life to the stage! *(Larry turns back to the partners.)* The other great thing Garry, that's important for all of us to note here, is that even though you were in the midst of this tremendous emotional response to your circumstance, you were continually aware of what Louise was giving to you and you worked off of her fully. In fact, out of your availability to her, she actually took you deeper into the reality of the imaginary great news that brought you home today. And this is exactly where so many actors fall into that ugly emotional trap of having their own emotional experience without any connection to their partners on stage or to anything going on in their environment. I'm talking about those actors who just love emotionally masturbating in front of the audience – it's not a pretty sight. It is essential, no matter what we are experiencing on stage, that we are absolutely and completely available and responsive to our partners and to our environment in every moment.

Kim: *(sitting in the third row next to Mercedes)* That really was thrilling to see. *(Mercedes is shaking her head in agreement.)*

Larry: Yes, it was. Now Louise, what was your experience, how was that for you.

Louise: It was such fun. It was almost overwhelming to be with Garry when he was so moved and so excited. It was like a wild roller-coaster ride.

Larry: And you did a beautiful job of going for that ride and working off Garry every moment. Also, your working off of him was simple and unforced and because of that, as I said, the exercise really took on a very lovely sense of reality. *(Larry turns to the class.)* Isn't that true?

Mercedes: Yeah, I knew they were doing repetition but, at the same time, I almost forgot that they were doing repetition. It was more like they were really in this wild thing together. I really forgot it was an exercise, that was so cool.

Larry: Thats right, they really moved away from "hey, let's do a good exercise," and they lived out this event in their room without trying to control it or manipulate it in anyway. And you see, now the repetition becomes freer. I'm almost afraid to say that because I do not mean in any way that you start having casual conversations. No! What I mean is that you must work off of each other much more closely, intuitively, and you must be more available to what is really happening in each moment. Well, that's enough for today. Thank you all for your work.

Session Three, Exercise Two

Please take at least a day to set up another exercise. After you have done the exercise, use the following page to do your journal work. When you have completed that, move on to the next session.

S e s s i o n F o u r

bringing back
the activity

Setup

In this exercise one partner is in the room with
an activity. The activity is physically difficult and
extremely meaningful.

The other partner goes out to do an emotional
preparation based on something that has just
happened or that he or she has just found out —
which is extremely meaningful. When you are
fully prepared, you come home to do something.

The relationship is roommates.

Instructions

In this exercise, we are bringing back the kind of activity you worked with in *Workbook One*. Which means that

the person who is "in the room" must have an activity that is, physically, very difficult to do — but not impossible to do. Remember? If you actually know that it is impossible to accomplish, why would you really bother and try to do it. You wouldn't. So make it extremely physically difficult. The other crucial element is that the reason you are doing it must be extremely meaningful.

Now the other partner will go out and do a full preparation. Then this partner will come home "to do" something which is in response to the imaginary circumstances that he or she has prepared from.

Also, the CIRCUMSTANCE that the partner who is outside is preparing FROM and the CIRCUMSTANCE the partner in the room has based his/her activity ON must be DIFFERENT. Is that clear? You are not including your "roommate" in the circumstances that you are working with.

Logistically, it is a good idea for the person in the room to keep the door open until she or he is ready to begin the exercise. In this way, if the person outside comes and sees the door open, they will know to go away and keep preparing until the person in the room is ready. If they come and see the door is shut, they know that they may come into the room. For the person in the room, make sure that you remember to close the door when you are ready to work or you will keep your partner stuck out there preparing and the exercise will never begin.

Okay, go ahead and put all of the elements together and when you are ready, do your exercise. Then, after writing your notes here in the book, read on.

Example Exercise: Donny and Ruthie

Larry: Ruthie, what was the activity?

Ruthie: *(Ruthie is talking very quietly.)* I was cutting the material for an outfit I designed.

Larry: You're embarrassed to talk about it.

Ruthie: *(Ruthie laughs)* Well, yeah, now that the exercise is over, I am very embarrassed.

Larry: Listen, that was very specific and wonderful work. Do you want to tell us why you were putting the outfit together?

Ruthie: Oh God, yeah, I can tell you. I mean, after this exercise, I'm sure it's no big mystery. I was cutting the material for an outfit I am going to wear at my new job dancing at a strip club.

Larry: That was very specific Ruthie and it really took on a very meaningful life for you. *(Larry turns to the class.)* Wish fulfillment. Do you all remember that? We can't deny our own fantasy life — doesn't mean you're gonna go be a stripper now. But when we start to really tie the activities into our own and personal fantasy life, what we may not allow ourselves to experience in our day-to-day lives, it opens up something for us in terms of aliveness and passion. *(Larry turns back to Ruthie.)* Now, that really freed up something very new for you, didn't it Ruthie.

Ruthie: Yeah... *(She laughs again.)* God, I am just so embarrassed.

Larry: I didn't know you were such a good dancer.

Ruthie: Well, I'm not trained or anything but I love to dance more than just about anything.

Larry: That's great and your working with Donny was excellent as well. I want you to notice that as the activity really took on a deepened meaning for you, not only were you trying to accomplish it at one hundred percent, you were absolutely available to Donny. I want you to know that your wide-open responsiveness is a direct result of how hard you worked to lay the groundwork; how hard you worked on all the repetition and activity work we did from way back at the beginning of the year. What you are discovering, in a profound way, is that the repetition is so clearly not about the words. It's about getting out of the way and doing what you have to do because you have no choice. That's a beautiful thing I am seeing in your work — you getting fully out of your own way.

Mandy: *(raising her hand from her seat in the second row)* Larry, I want to ask something about something you just talked about.

Larry: Yes Mandy.

Mandy: I'm not sure exactly what my question is... umm, could you talk a little more about the activity and our fantasy life.

Larry: What I am saying is that there are things we would all just love to do, dream of doing, dream of experiencing, wish we were capable of doing or wish we were free enough to do. And, in our lives, for whatever reason, we just don't do these things. Now, these are juicy avenues to explore, you know? Have I told you that if there were anything else in the world I could do, there are two of them I would give almost anything to be: a professional basketball player with the abilities of a Michael Jordan and a black gospel singer. Now, I could create some great activities based on my very deep connection to how much I wish I could stand up in a church, open my mouth and have some powerful black gospel sounds come out of me. That is a very delicious fantasy for me.

Mandy: So you are saying that the circumstance you create, and then the activity, must have a connection to your own wish fulfillment.

Larry: I am saying that the reason must always be extremely meaningful and that a great source is your hidden and censored desires. Look, our work-space is a safe place to explore these things. I mean, I wouldn't sing black gospel in front of just anyone. But doing it here, will do something to me. To be very clear, you always want the activity to support the reason you have set up so that the activity itself, and the doing of it, takes you further into the meaning of the imaginary circumstance. Now, whatever reason you are using, don't you think there's going to be a bigger payoff if the activity really turns you on to do? The answer is, yes it will. You know, you're the one who's choosing what you are going to have to do — why not make it something that is compelling for you to get involved in.

Mandy: Yeah, that makes sense.

Larry: Okay, Donny, tell us what the circumstance you prepared from was.

Donny: My Grandma called me screaming on the phone to get over to her house. And, I just came from her house where they just came and took away the body of my Grandfather who... my Grandfather who just... Goddammit! Goddammit! *(Donny is yelling.)* Son of a Bitch! *(He stands up and kicks the couch and walks over and leans on the wall.)* Goddammit! *(He kicks the wall and kneels down and starts to cry.)*

Larry: *(Larry talks quietly to Ruthie.)* Ruthie, go over and work off Donny right now, go ahead.

> *Ruthie goes to Donny. She kneels down beside him and is quiet. Donny has his two hands covering his face as he cries.*

Donny: *(whispering)* No, no, no, no....

Ruthie: You are in such pain.

Donny: I am in pain, Oh God, No!

Ruthie: *(She takes one of his hands from his face and he turns to her and hugs her tightly. Ruthie starts to cry with him.)* I am so sorry, I'm so sorry...

Donny: Don't let go.

Ruthie: I won't let go.

Donny: *(They hold each other. After a while, Donny begins to calm and he relaxes his grip on Ruthie.)* My nose is running on your shoulder.

Ruthie: That's all right.

Donny: *(laughs)* Doesn't look so good.

Ruthie: It's been worse. *(They look at each other and laugh together.)*

Larry: Okay guys, I want you to come back and sit on the couch, would you do that please?

Donny: Yeah... *(Donny and Ruthie stand slowly and go back to the couch. They sit and Larry waits for a few moments.)* Oh shit. Oh shit. *(He has his eyes closed and he is shaking his head.)* Oh man, now I get it.

Larry: What do you get.

Donny: This preparation stuff, shit, this is powerful shit. Oh man, this... man, I don't know...

Larry: Can you tell us what it is that you understand now.

Donny: Yeah, yeah... When I started to tell you what my imaginary circumstance was, something happened in a flash that didn't happen in the whole damn twenty minutes I was out there trying to prepare. It wasn't even an image or a thought, it was somehow in telling you about it, that made the whole thing just too damn real... Whew! Does that make sense, in the telling you about it?

Larry: Yes, that makes perfect sense. I'll share something with you. When I was learning this work at the Neighborhood Playhouse, I landed on the same discovery that you made just now. I don't remember exactly how it happened, but I do remember being out in the hall preparing and grabbing a student from another class who was walking through the hall and trying to tell her what was upsetting me. I didn't tell her "about" the imaginary circumstance, no, I spoke to this girl as if my circumstance was true and was happening "right now." I couldn't even get many words out of my mouth because as I tried to tell her, the meaning of the circumstance became so real for me, and so quickly, that I just left her there so I could "get home." "Home," of course, being the room and the exercise. By the way, one of the great things about the Playhouse was the respect all the students had for each other and for the intense demands of the work. We walked up and down the stairs very quietly because there was always someone crouched in a corner somewhere trying to prepare for an exercise. Fortunately, for me, this girl that I grabbed to talk with as I was preparing, simply listened to me. I still remember her being so available to me that, as I became extremely upset in sharing with her, there were tears streaming down her face. That thing, trying to talk to someone about the circumstance as I was preparing, was so powerful and so persuasive for me, that I kept exploring it in many ways. I discovered that I could also prepare effectively being in public rather than in some dark little space by myself. So, I would go outside to do my preparation and just walking in the midst of strangers on the street became a great tool for taking on the reality of the imaginary circumstances. Sometimes, I would go around the corner from the Playhouse to this deli and, like I did with the girl in the hall of the Playhouse, I would try to tell the guy behind the counter about my circumstance as if it was actually happening. I remember once telling him something incredibly exciting that I was preparing about and how happy he got for me.

Mercedes: *(sitting in the seat next to Larry)* You mean you actually spoke to this deli guy as if your imaginary circumstance was real?

Larry: Yep. I did it in the deli, I did it with the guys who cooked the burgers in the greasy-spoon we all ate lunch in, I did it with people who were walking on the street. I never had to say very much, it was more about simply trying to tell them, that made the whole thing so real for me. And, I didn't always prepare that way – but I had found something that worked and I kept trying it out in every imaginable way. You know, there was another important discovery I made out of all that. When I prepared by myself, I started to write letters to family members or friends about the circumstances I was preparing from as if they were true. Again, trying to write my fantasy down in the form of a letter to someone I loved, was very effective for me.

Mercedes: So you had stuff to write on with you when you went out to prepare?

Larry: Always. It might just be some little scratch pad I kept stuffed in my pocket or, depending on the circumstances I was setting up, I might go out and buy a special greeting card that fit the meaning of what I was preparing about.

Mercedes: God, I never even thought about that kind of stuff.

Larry: It's something I keep saying about this emotional preparation work. You will keep teaching yourself how to do it in the doing of it. And, each one of us must find our own "way in," our own approach that works for us. You try "this." If "this" doesn't work, try "that." If "that" works, use it. And if it suddenly doesn't work, in that moment, let it go and find something else. Keep exploring and stay open. *(Larry turns back to Donny.)* Can you talk a little more about your circumstance?

Donny: Yeah, I came from my Grandma's house where they took away the body of my Grandpa who had just committed suicide.

Larry: And what were you coming home to do.

Donny: Well, my Grandpa was a moving man, he moved furniture. He and his brothers had their own moving company But they got older and now the company is gone. Not working anymore has made my Grandpa pretty depressed. So, I decided that the oldest brother was supposed to pay my Grandpa a large some of money that was due to my Grandpa for his share of the moving truck that they sold. But, the oldest brother who ran the company and who is kind of a slimy character, took the money and ran. My Grandpa was counting on this money to live on and when he found out that his brother stole the money, my Grandpa hung himself.

Larry: That's a very powerful circumstance Donny, and what did you come home to do.

Donny: I came home with the rope that... that my Grandpa used to hang himself and I was trying to write on the rope with a marker how I felt about the brother who, basically, killed him.

Larry: That's just fantastic Donny — very, very specific. And you uncovered a whole new possibility for your preparations today. The other thing I want to give you high praise for is that, although you never got to the deeper meaning that this circumstance has for you during the exercise, you didn't try to push the emotion or try to make it look like you had something going on that wasn't going on. *(Larry turns to the class.)* Do you remember what you call trying to make it look like you have something going on for you that really isn't?

Kristin: That's indication.

Larry: Right. Indicating is trying to show what isn't really happening for you. I know I've said this a hundred times and I want you to hear it again. Indicating emotion is a lie and it always communicates to the audience as false. It is a horrible trap actors fall into and it is an ugly habit. It's also the easy way out because most actors aren't interested in or willing to pay the price and work for real. When an actor indicates, no matter how slick the actor — and there are a lot of very slick actors — the audience knows in their gut that something is wrong here; they have to shut off a part of themselves so that they can just sit through the performance — and they have thoughts like, "oh yeah, this is just theatre anyway." But when an actor works for real, as we know from witnessing the work in this room, the reality of the life in front of us is breathtaking and riveting.

Nancy: So what do you do if you are supposed to come into a scene absolutely heartbroken and your preparation didn't work and you have to be out on stage right now?

Larry: Great question. Anybody want to answer that question?

Patrick: Accept where you are at.

Larry: That's right! You must always accept where you are at, what is really happening for you. First of all, if you don't accept it, if you don't embrace what is really happening, you will shut yourself off from the possibility of anything real happening for you at all. You will also shut yourself off from your partner on stage. The beauty is, when you embrace where you are at and turn yourself over to your partner, they will feed you so much that you will get to where you need to be by working off of them. You know, this kind of acceptance in each moment keeps you loose and agile and honest. Also, you must remember that the audience doesn't come in with any kind of particular emotional demands on you. If you accept what's going on fully, they will too. Okay guys, thanks. A lot of learning today, I love it.

Session Four, Exercise Two

Please take at least a day to set up another exercise. After you have done the exercise, use the space below to do your journal work. When you have completed that, move on to the next session.

_____

_____

_____

_____

_____

_____

_____

_____

_____

_____

_____

_____

_____

_____

_____

_____

_____

_____

_____

both partners prepare

Setup

In this exercise, both people are fully preparing.

You are no longer "roommates." Choose a relationship in which you do not live together.

The partner "in the room" will go out and do a full preparation. As always, the preparation comes out of imaginary circumstances, based on an element of truth that is extremely meaningful! He or she will then come home "to do" out of that preparation. (So the activity need not be physically difficult any longer. Again, the difficulty is now an emotional one.)

The other partner will go out and do a full preparation. When ready, he or she will come and knock on the door.

The reasons both people prepare from, must have nothing to do with the other partner in the exercise.

Instructions

I think this is pretty clear. Both partners must go out and take their time to do a full preparation. Keep the door open until the partner who's room it is comes in to get going on the thing they have come home "to do." (For this partner, remember to close that door so that the person who is coming "to knock" knows when you are ready to work.) Also, I repeat myself, it is important that the reasons you are working with are not about the other person in the relationship you have chosen.

Go ahead and put all of the elements together and when you are ready, do your exercise. Then, after writing your notes here in the book, read on.

_____

_____

_____

_____

_____

_____

_____

Please Note!

From this point on in the book, rather than giving you my comments to the invented students after the invented exercise, I am going to give you an example of a successful exercise by sharing with you a "transcript" of the invented exercise itself. After this playback of the exercise, I will have the "students" tell us how they set up the elements of the exercise for themselves.

Example Exercise: Ralph and Alice

(Ralph comes into the room and shuts the door gently. He has full clown makeup on his face, painted with a huge purple-lipped smile and wide eyes. He wears a long raincoat and on his feet, long floppy red clown shoes. Behind all the makeup, Ralph is distraught and seems not to have even enough energy to stand on his feet. He walks slowly to the desk and pulls a small tape recorder out of a drawer. He takes it to the sofa, throws it down on a pillow and takes off his raincoat. Ralph is wearing a bright orange and yellow clown costume with a big silver sword on his side. He tries to sit but the handle of the sword jabs him in his side, so he pulls the sword out of his belt and throws it at the wall. Now he sits down and takes a cassette tape out of the raincoat pocket and unwraps it. He puts the tape into the tape recorder and presses a button. He puts the recorder near his mouth but has difficulty talking.)

Ralph: Dear...Dear Mr. Williams. My name is Ralph...OH SHIT!

(Ralph stands and stops the recorder from taping. He carries the recorder as he walks towards the bed. His face is tight and his empty hand is clenched into a fist. He looks up at the ceiling and screams.)

Ralph: YOU FUCKING BASTARD I HATE YOU AAAAHHH-HH I HATE YOU SO MUCH!

(Ralph falls on the bed into a fetal position and clutches the blanket to his stomach. After a while, he pulls the recorder to his mouth and switches it on again.)

Ralph: Dear Mr. Williams. I am a friend of your son, Billy. Do you remember him? There are some imporant things you need to hear. First I want you to hear what...

(There is a loud knock on Ralph's door. We hear an excited Alice yelling from outside the room, rapidly rapping and tapping on the door.)

Alice: Ralphie, Ralphie, Ralphie, Ralphie, Ralphie! I did it, I did it, I did it, YAAAHOOOOOOO!

(Ralph clicks off the tape recorder and puts the blanket over his head. He stays that way, saying nothing.)

Alice: *(banging on the door)* Ralphie, oh Ralphie, please be home, are you home? Are you, huh, are you? *(She continues to knock loudly on the door.)*

Ralph: *(yells from under the blanket)* Quit the fucking knocking will you!

Alice: You are home! Come on Ralphie, let me in, let me in.

Ralph: *(He throws down the blanket and stands up as he yells again.)* Okay, just quit the damn knocking. *(Ralph walks towards the door.)*

Alice: Come on Ralphie, don't be in a bad mood, not now. Just open the door, will ya!

Ralph: *(He opens the door.)*

Alice: *(She laughs hysterically.)* Oh my God, you're a clown!

Ralph: I sure am.

Alice: *(Grabs Ralphs hand and tries to make him dance with her as she laughs.)* You're a clown, you're a clown, you're a clown, you're a...

Ralph: Quit pushing me around.

Alice*: (She throws her arms around Ralph and gives him a big bear hug.)* I'M NOT PUSHY, I'M HAPPY! *(Alice leaps around the room.)* I'M HAPPY, I'M SNAPPY, I'M HAPPY, I'M SNAPPY, I AM HAPPY!

Ralph: Yeah, you're happy all right.

Alice: *(laughing)* You just want to bring me down you clown.

Ralph: *(He closes the door.)* Yeah I just want to bring you down.

Alice: Oh come on Ralphie, don't placate me.

Ralph: Quit calling me Ralphie, I hate that.

Alice: Boy, you really don't like that.

Ralph: Keen observer, aren't you.

Alice: Shit! Don't be sarcastic with me Ralphie boy.

Ralph: You did it again!

Alice: Woops! Ralph, Ralph, you're name is Ralph.

Ralph: I don't have time for this Alice. *(He has sat back down on the bed and is holding the tape recorder.)*

Alice: Oh maaaan, I am supposed to be happy. Come on, please, be happy with me Ralph.

Ralph: I can't be happy with you right now.

Alice: You are so down.

Ralph: *(looking down at the recorder on his lap, speaks quietly now)* I'm sorry.

Alice: You're sorry.

Ralph: Yeah, I'm sorry. *(He starts to cry.)* Oh shit...

Alice: *(She sits next to him on the bed and puts her arm around his shoulders.)* I forgive you.

Ralph: Thank you.

Alice: You're welcome.

Ralph: You are so sweet:

Alice: I'm sweet?

Ralph: Yeah you are.

Alice: I am not sweet.

Ralph: Yeah, you are.

Alice: No, I'm not sweet, clown man.

Ralph: Stop arguing with me, you're sweet damn it! *(They look at each other, and they both laugh.)*

Alice: You are right, I'M SWEET! You're such a goon.

Ralph: Man, you are just beaming with happiness.

Alice: I am so happy Ralph.

Ralph: I'm glad for you.

Alice: You are, really?

Ralph: Yes I am. *(He looks at the recorder again. It is still in his left hand.)*

Alice: There's something going on with this tape player and you.

Ralph: Yes, there is something going on. *(He gets upset again)*

Alice: Oh no, oh no, you're really upset about it.

Ralph: I am upset about it.

Alice: I'm so sorry Ralph.

Ralph: Look, I can't do this with you here.

Alice: It's private.

Ralph: Yeah, it's private. *(He breaks down. Alice goes to hug him. He stands and backs up to the wall as he speaks.)* NO! NO! Please don't! Please go, I really have to do this now.

Alice: OH GOD, You are in such pain.

Ralph: Yes, please go, I need you to go. I need you to go now!

(Alice doesn't say anything. She walks out and shuts the door behind her. Ralph kicks the couch hard five times and clicks on the recorder and yells into it.)

Ralph: You motherfucker where the hell were you today, he needed you there, he kept saying my daddy loves me my daddy loves me and all I could say was yes he does, I kept trying to look him in the eyes and say yes he does and I was so full of shit because you don't give a damn, what kind of animal are you not to be there today you piece of shit, I want to kill you for what you did to him, oh God how could you do this to him oh God oh God oh God, I hurt...I hurt...I hurt...I am sick...you make me so sick...

(Ralph's whole body is shaking. His hands are trembling. He tries to shut the recorder off. He can't get it to shut off and suddenly, with tremendous force, he throws it down on the floor where it smashes into pieces. He yells at it, "Fuck you! Fuck you!" and he goes under the table to get the cassette tape which has landed there. He picks up the tape and runs out of the room.)

. . .

The following is what Ralph and Alice said to me as they explained how they set up the circumstances from which they prepared:

Ralph: Well, I've been doing volunteer work at the Children's Hospital. I go in and read stories to the kids. There's this one kid Billy, who is real sick and, I don't know, I was an only child and I always wished I had a brother and he's become like a little brother to me. Billy's mom died last year and he has said some things about his father to me and I get a sense that his father isn't, well, to be generous, he doesn't sound like a great guy.

I set up the circumstances... I decided that the hospital called me to come in right away because they know how close Billy and I have gotten and they told me that he wasn't going to make it through the night. I have just come from the hospital where I was with Billy. I was with him as he died and that, though his father wasn't even there to be with him, he kept telling me how much his father really loved him. And those were the last words he spoke, that his daddy loves him. I also added that the nurse told me that they did get the father on the phone and they advised him of Billy's condition, but that the father said he had a business trip that he couldn't cancel.

Out of that, I decided that I was coming home to make a tape recording of what happened, what Billy said as he died and how I felt about the father. I was going to go back to the hospital to get the father's address so I could go put the tape in his mailbox.

Oh yeah, I was wearing the clown costume because, when the hospital called, I had just spent the day there at the hospital entertaining the kids with my clown and sword routine. It's about a clown who wishes he was a pirate. They love the act and, in actuality, Billy loves when I come dressed in my clown get-up.

Alice: Ralph forgot to say that our relationship was business partners. We had just started a graphic design company.

My circumstance was that I just found out that, after trying to get a grant to start a shelter for battered women for the last three years, I just received word that this time, I was awarded the largest grant ever given by the county for this kind of service! That's what I prepared from.

Session Five, Exercise Two

Please take at least a day to set up another exercise. After you have done the exercise, use the following page to do your journal work. When you have completed that, move on to the next session.

_____

_____

_____

_____

_____

_____

_____

_____

_____

_____

_____

_____

_____

_____

_____

_____

_____

_____

_____

it's about the partner

Setup

In this exercise, both people are fully preparing.

Again, choose a relationship in which you do not live together.

The partner "in the room" will go out and do a full preparation. He or she will then come home "to do" out of that preparation.

The other partner will go out and do a full preparation. When ready, he or she will come and knock on the door.

**The reason that the person "in the room" pre-
pares from, must have nothing to do with the
other partner in the exercise.**

**The reason that the person "coming to the door"
prepares from, must be about or include the
other partner in the exercise.**

Instructions

The set up for this exercise is the same as our previous
exercise, with one change. In the last exercise, the person
coming to the door was doing a preparation out of a circumstance which had nothing to do with the partner in the
room. NOW – IT DOES! Now, the person coming to the
door prepares out of an extremely meaningful circumstance that is specifically about or specifically includes the
partner in the room.

As we add this element in the exercise, I want to
remind the person coming to the door of an essential thing
to remember as you set up your circumstance. (I say
remind because, if you recall, we dealt with this same issue
in *Workbook One*.) The circumstance must be about or
include the partner in the room – AND – it must be
extremely meaningful to who? TO YOU! First and fore-
most, it must have deep meaning to you and then, it must
be about or include your partner. Now you see how carefully you must choose the relationship the two of you will
be working with.

So that you are absolutely clear, here's an example of a
not so great reason:

> **Bonnie and Paul decide the relationship will be sister and brother. Bonnie is coming to the door. Bonnie's reason is that she has just found out that her brother Paul sexually molested a young woman.**

Why do I say that this reason isn't a great one? The answer is that it doesn't go far enough in it's specificity; in how it is specifically connected to Bonnie. Now, I happen to know something you don't. I know that in reality, Bonnie has a daughter in high school. Take a look at how I reworked the same reason by making it more specific in it's meaning to Bonnie:

> **Bonnie and Paul decide the relationship will be sister and brother. Bonnie is coming to the door. Bonnie's reason is that she has just come from the hospital where her high-school daughter is in a coma after being beat up and raped. The doctors are not optimistic about her chances of survival. At the hospital, Bonnie's daughter's best friend Jodi was there. Jodi was also beat up by the same man but she got away before being raped. Jodi told Bonnie that she was afraid to tell the police who did it because the man warned the two girls that if they spoke up, he'd come for Jodi's little sister with a gun. But, at the hospital, Jodi broke down and told Bonnie that the man who attacked them was Bonnie's brother Paul.**

Now, do you see how that is more extreme – specifically – and more personally engaging for Bonnie? Yes, it is. Now she has something to prepare from and which brings her to Paul's door with tremendous urgency. Remember, the reason must always have deep meaning to you or else there is nothing to work from.

Go ahead and put all of the elements together and when you are ready, do your exercise. Then, after writing your notes here in the book, read on.

_____

_____

_____

_____

_____

_____

_____

_____

_____

_____

_____

_____

_____

_____

_____

_____

_____

_____

_____

_____

_____

Example Exercise: Wilma and Fred

(Fred comes storming into the room mumbling under his breath, "...stupid motherfucker." He throws his briefcase down on the sofa and goes back to slam the door closed. He rips off his grey sport jacket and throws it on the sofa as he opens the briefcase and pulls out some papers, magazines and a journal notebook. He puts these on the round oak table. Then, Fred goes to the closet and brings out a typewriter which he puts on the same table and plugs the machine into the wall outlet. He kicks off his shoes and sits down to put a blank sheet of paper into the typewriter. The first piece doesn't go in straight and Fred tears it out, crumples it up and throws it at the wall yelling, "FUCK YOU!" Fred hears some footsteps near his door, he remains very quiet and looks at the door and waits. Nothing happening out there, so he puts another piece in more carefully and then he turns the machine on. He thinks for a few moments and then he types a few words down on the page. He re-reads what he wrote for a minute, isn't satisfied and he pulls the page out, crumples it and throws it at the wall. Again, Fred puts a piece of white paper into the typewriter, looks for the words in his mind and then types a sentence. Suddenly, there is very loud pounding on his door. It stops. Fred sits silently and waits. Then, the pounding begins again and, this time, with each crash on the door, we hear Wilma yell...)

Wilma: YOU! OPEN! THIS! DOOR!

(Fred remains quiet, pretending no one is at home. Wilma gets louder, this time kicking the door.)

Wilma: I heard you typing, you slime. OPEN THE DOOR!

(Fred is panicked and frozen and unsure what to do.)

Wilma: I'll just stand here and scream until you let me in you bastard. *(She screams over and over.)* OPEN THE DOOR! OPEN THE DOOR! OPEN THE DOOR! OPEN THE DOOR!...

(As Wilma continues yelling, Fred gets up and grabs a blanket that was on the sofa and throws it over the whole table of things he was just working with. He runs to the door and opens it. As he grabs Wilma's arm and pulls her into the room, he yells at her.)

Fred: Get the hell in here!

Wilma: Keep your stinking hands off me!

Fred: Just shut your damn mouth.

(Wilma suddenly leaps at Fred and grabs him by the shoulders and starts shaking him with tremendous force.)

Wilma: I will kill you, you animal.

(Fred gets himself loose from her grip and backs away.)

Fred: You are sick.

Wilma: I'm sick?

Fred: Yes you are.

Wilma: I'll show you how sick I am!

(Wilma begins to destroy Fred's room — throwing chairs, knocking over the bookcase, kicking books, etc. Fred is trying to stop her but she will not be stopped. Finally, she pulls the blanket off of the table and as she knocks the typewriter to the floor...)

Fred: DON'T TOUCH IT, NOOOOOOOO!

Wilma: *(laughing hysterically)* Oh boy, that touched a nerve.

Fred: *(putting the typewriter back on the table)* How can you be so mean.

Wilma: *(still laughing)* You ain't seen nothin yet!

Fred: *(picking up the magazines and journal from the floor)* Bitch!

Wilma: *(Her laughing has now turned into loud sobs as she cries.)* Name Calling? That the best you can do you asshole. *(She grabs the magazine out of Fred's hand.)* Porno? Porno? You filthy slob.

Fred: You don't know what the hell you're talking about.

Wilma: *(She starts jabbing him in the chest with the magazine.)* I know what I'm talking about you slimy creep.

Fred: *(He knocks the magazine out of her hand, grabs her by the shoulders and pins her up against the wall. He yells in her face with incredible intensity.)* What is your problem!!

Wilma: *(She is shaking and sobbing and can't speak. Fred continues to hold her against the wall. Finally, in a whisper...)* You killed Shane.

Fred: I killed Shane?

Wilma: Don't you play dumb with me.

Fred: I am not playing dumb.

Wilma: You sold Shane to the lab and they killed him.

Fred: No, I didn't do that.

Wilma: *(screams)* Don't play innocent with me!

Fred: *(screams back)* I'm not playing innocent, I DID NOT DO IT!

Wilma: You didn't?

(Fred shakes his head.)

Wilma: *(She breaks away from Fred's hold.)* Oh my God...

Fred : *(He runs after her, takes her arms and turns her to him.)* Wilma, I would never do that, never.

Wilma: You really didn't? *(She studies his eyes.)*

Fred: I DIDN'T!

Wilma: Oh God, you didn't!

(Wilma collapses in Fred's arms and cries. He holds her tightly.)

Wilma: Shane is dead, he's dead.

Fred: I'm so sorry.

Wilma: He's gone.

Fred: I'm so sorry for you, Wilma.

Wilma: *(She opens her eyes and sees the room over Fred's shoulder.)* I wrecked your room.

Fred: Yeah, you did.

Wilma: I am so ashamed, I am so ashamed.

(Wilma runs out of the room. Fred runs to the door.)

Fred: Wait.

(Wilma is gone. Fred closes the door and turns to the room. He looks at the mess and slides down the door until he is sitting on the floor. He begins to cry and he calls out...)

Fred: HANNAH! HANNAH! OH GOD HANNAH!

(Fred gets up and gets the typewriter set up to get back to work. Once again, he takes a blank sheet of paper and puts it into the typewriter. He thinks and then he types with powerful strokes.)

. . .

The following is what Wilma and Fred said to me as they explained how they set up the circumstances from which they prepared:

Wilma: Our relationship is that Fred and I were married for ten years and we got divorced two months ago. My circumstance was that my dog Shane, has been missing for the last week. I never had children and Shane has really been like my child for the last eight years. I've put up posters all over town but nobody has reported seeing Shane.

I just came from Bob's house, who is also a good friend of my ex-husband Fred. Bob said that he had to tell me, although he promised Fred to keep it a secret, that Fred came back into my house, took Shane and sold him to a lab for medical experimentation where, after their tests, they put Shane to sleep.

Also, as you advised when we did the first round of these exercises earlier in the year, (see *Workbook One*) before the exercise began, I told Fred three things I wanted him to know. I told him that I had begun guitar lessons, that I have had a dog named Shane for eight years now, and that I was getting a new job.

Fred: My reason was that I was just fired from my job. The thing that makes this really bad right now is that I was just about to get onto the company medical insurance plan. And, my boss, who is a real bastard anyway, fired me for a stupid little reason. Anyway, the reason it's the worst time in the world for me to get fired is that my new wife, Hannah, has just been diagnosed with cervical cancer and we have no insurance. I absolutely must keep my job and get on this insurance plan, I begged my boss to let me keep my job but he laughed at me and said, "tough luck."

I came home to write an extremely sexually explicit letter that I am going to send to three female employees who my boss has been hitting on at work. After I type the letters, I'm going to forge his signature on them. I am also putting pornographic pictures from magazines into a little journal that I am going to put in a place by his desk where I know one of the women, his secretary, will find it. I'm gonna get his ass fired and maybe even taken to court, and I'm going to ruin his name in the industry.

Session Six, Exercise Two

Please take at least a day to set up another exercise. After you have done the exercise, use the following page to do your journal work. When you have completed that, move on to the next session.

the highest stakes

Setup

In this exercise, both people are fully preparing.

Again, choose a relationship in which you do not live together.

The partner "in the room" will go out and do a full preparation. He or she will then come home "to do" out of that preparation.

The other partner will go out and do a full preparation. When ready, he or she will come and knock on the door.

The reason that the person "in the room" pre-pares from, must not be about the other partner in the exercise.

The reason that the person "coming to the door" prepares from, must be about or include the other partner in the exercise.

The person "in the room" will also add some-thing, in the extreme, that has just happened or that they have just found out that is about or includes the partner. This thing that you add MUST NOT BE RELATED to what you are coming home to do out of your preparation.

Instructions

Once again, we are taking the exercise from the previ-ous session and adding one new element to it. (This is the final element we will be adding to the exercise.) This time, the new element is for the person whose room it is. This can be a little confusing, so let me make it very clear.

The person in the room will go out and do a full prepa-ration based on an extreme circumstance. Out of that preparation, he or she will come home "to do" something. In addition, this person will add something that is extreme-ly meaningful that is specifically about or includes the other partner, the other person in the relationship.

Also, and importantly, the thing that the partner "in the room" adds about the person "coming to the door" must not be connected to what you are preparing from. For example, let's take Fred's from the previous session. If he was doing this new element, he would still have the preparation based on getting fired from his job at the worst possible time because of Hannah's illness. Then, in addition to that circumstance, he might add something like this:

Fred's mother has been severely depressed since Fred and Alice's divorce because of her son losing the marriage and because of how much she loved her daughter-in-law Alice. She even made a suicide attempt, which is why she is in the hospital right now. Fred's mom has just called him and said that Alice visited her today and Alice made it clear that she wanted very much to remain close friends with her. She even set up a lunch date for the following week. Fred's mom was laughing on the phone and sounded more optimistic about her life than Fred had heard in the past two months.

So you see, now Fred has a very specific thing that brings him home "to do" (his circumstance about getting fired and Hannah being ill), and he has a very specific point of view towards Alice. Alice is no longer just "Alice the ex-wife." NOW she is Alice who just saved his mother's life! This imaginary reason he created about Alice and his mom works in terms of the relationship they set up, AND it has an element of truth, which makes it deeply meaningful to Fred. That element of truth is how much Fred truly cares about his mother and her well-being.

As we get into working with this element, you may wonder, "Well, which thing do I prepare from — the circumstance that brings me home 'to do' something, or the circumstance I've added about my partner?" It's a good question. Here is my suggestion:

Always prepare from the circumstance out of which you are coming home "to do" something. It's important, before you do your emotional preparation, to remind yourself of the circumstance you have added about your partner, but then leave it alone. Trust that you know it. If you set it up well, when you see the other person, it will have an impact on you that will be out of your control. And that's exactly what you want. Now you will be in very specific response to the other person because of the meaning you have given to him or her out of the circumstance you created that involves them.

So, back to Fred for a moment. When Fred goes out to get ready to begin the exercise, he would remind himself first about how wonderful Alice was to help lift his mother's spirits. Then he leaves that alone and he would begin preparing about getting fired by his low-life boss at this time when he desperately needs to keep his job due to Hannah's illness. This preparation brings him home "to do" the forged letter and the rest of his activity. Then, if his ex-wife Alice should come over to his house, he will know exactly how he feels about her.

Is that clear now? Okay, time to get to work. Go ahead and put all of the elements together and when you are ready, do your exercise. Then, after writing your notes here in the book, read on.

Please Note!

In this session, rather than giving you a "transcript" of the invented exercise, I will give you two examples of exercises which include the newest element and which were set up well by the students.

Example One: Ann and Joy

The relationship is coworkers.

Ann is the partner "in the room."

Joy is the partner "coming to the door."

Ann: Since their divorce when I was seven, I have always wished that my parents would get back together. A few times, right after the divorce, I heard my mother crying so deeply in her room, I was sure her heart was going to crack open and she was going to die. When I asked her why they weren't together anymore, she said that they just couldn't make it work. I never knew what she meant and as I got older, she wouldn't discuss it. But she was never the same. I always remembered how much she laughed when I was real little and it makes me so incredibly sad when I think about how little she has laughed since the divorce.

The circumstance from which I prepared was that she just called me and told me that my father and her had seen each other a few times in the past month. She hadn't told me until today because she wasn't ready to talk about it. But now, she was all giddy on the phone and she sounded like a kid. She was calling to tell me that they are going to get remarried in a simple ceremony at her house at the end of this week.

I was coming home to learn my mom's favorite love song on the piano and to sing it, so that I can perform it at their wedding.

This is what I added about Joy. My relationship with Joy is that we are coworkers at a large computer software company. We are both in the marketing division and we are packaging designers. I just came from work where I found out from a good friend there, that Joy had been awarded a promotion based on the acceptance of her box design for a new educational CD-ROM — a project which I was the lead designer on. I have been working in the department for two years longer than Joy and that job was supposed to be mine. Getting a promotion there is extremely important to me right now because my husband and I bought our "dream house" based on the increased salary I was going to receive. Without it, there's no way we can afford the mortgage because my husband's company, another computer corporation, just went under. Also, when I saw Joy's design it looked very similar to mine and I know that she ripped off my ideas. I can't go to our superior and complain because he's dating Joy! And the superior above him is this guy's brother-in-law! So, basically, Joy screwed me big time!

Joy: There's this guy at work who I have been crazy about for the last year. Whenever I've talked with him, watched him be so generous with others, witnessed how gentle he is and kind to everyone, I knew that I could marry this guy. But I never let him know how I felt because I knew he was seriously involved with someone else.

The circumstance that I prepared from was that yesterday at work, I got an e-mail from this guy asking me if I would have coffee with him at the cafeteria. We did! And then we went to dinner after work and then we went to a movie and then we went to a cafe and talked for two hours! This morning there were flowers on my desk from him and a beautiful note saying he hasn't felt this happy in years. I just came from an early dinner with him at the company cafeteria (he had to work late) and he told me that it was my coworker Ann who knew he broke up with his girlfriend and suggested strongly to him that he give me a call!

(NOTE: As we have talked about before, sometimes there is information you need to tell your partner before you do the exercise so that if your reason should come out in the exercise, you will both be able to take on that reality from your own point of view. I want you to fill in the following blanks by writing down what you think Ann and Joy would have to tell each other.)

Ann tells Joy: _____

_____

_____

Joy tells Ann: _____

_____

_____

Example Two: Jimmy and Cathy

The relationship is neighbors.

Jimmy is the partner "in the room."

Cathy is the partner "coming to the door."

Jimmy: I am also a volunteer firefighter and I have a six-year-old son who lives with his mother in her house which is about five miles from my home. I have been so busy at work this last year...well, I certainly have tremendous guilt about not being with my son more often.

The circumstance from which I prepared is that I got a call last night from my ex-wife telling me that they had, of all things, a fire at her house and that the house was totally destroyed. This happened at the same time as I was out fighting a fire in another part of the city. She said that the firefighters got her out very quickly but it took them quite a while to find my son David. She also told me that David is in the hospital in intensive care and the doctors don't think he's going to make it. I went to the hospital and spent the night there.

I fell asleep in a chair in David's room and woke up to David saying he wanted two things: his toy firetruck and a piece of cake. The doctor was standing there with some charts and he told me with great delight that David has made tremendous progress. As I headed to the cafeteria to get some cake for David, the doctor stopped me in the hall and said that David should make full recovery within a few months.

On my way home, I went to see my ex-wife's house. When I was there I found David's favorite toy in the driveway — the metal firetruck that I gave to him when he was four and which he had just asked for at the hospital. It's all bent out of shape. I was coming home to make it look perfect again so I can bring it over to David.

My relationship with Cathy is neighbors. She has continually demanded me to chop down one of my trees which she says is on her property. This is a tree that my father planted when he first built the house and which I spent endless hours climbing and playing in when I grew up. I love that tree and it has so much meaning for me. I know that the tree is on my property and I have refused to cut it down. As I returned home just now, the tree was chopped down and there was this note in my mailbox from Cathy (he pulls the note out of his pocket) which says, "I had to take matters into my own hands! Your fed-up neighbor, Cathy"

Cathy: I know that Jimmy, besides being an actor-in-training, is also a volunteer firefighter. Working from our relationship as neighbors, my circumstance was that last night there was a fire in my mother's nursing home. Some of the residents were killed but my mother was saved by the firefighters. When I got the call last night from a security person at the nursing home about the fire, I drove there and found my mother in an ambulance being treated for some minor burns. This morning, I called the fire station to see if I could find out who actually carried my mother out of the building. They said they'd investigate and call me back.

Anyway, they just called and I just found out that it was my neighbor, Jimmy, who saved my mothers life! By the way, isn't that so weird how we both used such similar things... I mean about the fires and everything? I just think it's so amazing.

Jimmy tells Cathy: _____

_____

_____

Cathy tells Jimmy: _____

_____

_____

Session Seven, Exercise Two

Please take at least a day to set up another exercise. After you have done the exercise, use the following space to do your journal work. When you have completed that, move on to the next session.

_____

_____

_____

_____

_____

_____

_____

_____

_____

_____

what's next!

If you have gotten to this point by actually "doing" the book, I'm confident that you have learned some essential things about the heightened emotional demands the theatre makes of us. I also know that you have had to do some serious grappling with your own deeper point of view towards life and the world around you and how to become more freely the authentic expression of that point of view.

If you have reached this "wrap up" after simply reading the book, I hope you have found the information valuable and clear, and that it makes you want to go back to the exercises sometime and "get your hands dirty." Because the truth is, no matter how interesting this book may be, the only real knowledge available is in the doing of the work. If I have learned anything, it is that the real answers to all of our questions, the surprising and unimagined answers, are always and only to be found in the work itself.

As I mentioned early on, one of the traps of this work is the danger of becoming "emotion conscious." You see, it's a place I find most actors want to stop. Why? Because it feels good. You know, having our emotions is a great feeling, isn't it?

But, as I told you, acting is not emoting — it is doing. And so, you must understand very clearly for what purpose we have worked so hard on making powerful connection to our deeper truths. And, you must now learn what to *actively do* with it all. In fact, everything we have done together so far, in this book and in my *Meisner Workbook* that precedes it, has paved the way for you to begin to learn how to work with text, character and the more advanced aspects of interpretation.

So, This is where I plug my next book on the Meisner Approach, *Workbook Three: Tackling The Text.*

In *Workbook Three,* as you encounter the script for the first time, you will begin to experience how all the fundamental abilities you have been working on are essential if you are to truly bring the words to life. For the first time, you will discover in a most intimate way that acting is not really about the words. Clearly, the words must serve as our source of inspiration: they are the playwright's job. The actor's job is about really living on stage, it's about fighting for your life, it's about true and human behavior and what is happening between you and your partner — right now!

As in the first two books, when we start to work with text, I will be teaching you a specifically laid out process. In a step-by-step fashion, I will give you the tools that will lead you to transform the words on the page into a passionate and vital improvisation. You will see that in the scripted scene, you must be continually willing and able to give up your ideas of how you think the scene should be acted. And, I will consistently lead you away from the clichés of performance – all those preconcieved notions of how to deliver a line or in what way you think "a person like that" should act.

I will also begin to teach you how to look at the script *as an actor*. What does that mean? Basically, it means how to ask the right questions! You will learn the ways of talking to yourself that will first, enable you to understand the very personal desires of the character and then, help you make his or her deeply held needs your own. What I am talking about really, is taking our first steps into "interpretation," which will be explored in the last of my Meisner books, *Workbook Four: Interpretation*.

So, see you in *Workbook Three*. I can't wait to get to work with you on what I consider, the juiciest and tastiest parts of acting!

Stay well, Love Larry.

P.S. When Marisa, the "Smith" of Smith & Kraus Publishers, first read my manuscript for this book, she wondered, *"What happened to Tom, that student you asked to leave class, to take a long walk and to figure out if he really wanted to study this work?"* Remember him? Since Marisa was curious, I thought you all might like to know what happened with Tom. (As you know, I invented Tom and all of the students. So, I get to invent this too!) Well, although I had asked Tom to give me a decision that day about his continuing in class or not, he never came back to talk with me, he never called me and I haven't seen him since. But last week, Wilma, one of the other students in class, told me she saw him on TV and that Tom now has a leading role on a very popular daytime soap opera, *The Slim and the Shameless.*

Biography

Larry Silverberg, author of *The Sanford Meisner Approach: An Actor's Workbook, The Sanford Meisner Approach: Workbook Two — Emotional Freedom, Loving To Audition, The Actor's Guide to Qualified Acting Coaches: New York* and *The Actor's Guide to Qualified Acting Coaches: Los Angeles*, is a graduate of the Neighborhood Playhouse School of Theatre in New York City where he studied with master acting teacher Sanford Meisner. Since then, he has worked professionally as an actor and director throughout the United States and Canada in feature films, network television, Off-Broadway and regional theatre.

Larry also teaches professional acting classes at his own acting studio in Seattle and he has taught master classes in the Meisner work at universities, colleges and acting studios around the country. His students have gone on to work in television and feature films including: *Cape Fear, Making Mr. Right, Let It Ride, Miami Vice, Northern Exposure, B.L. Stryker, Miami Blues, Super Boy, Phantom of the Ritz, America's Most Wanted* and many others.

Larry offers visiting acting intensives and workshops. You may contact him with questions about teaching at your school or with questions about this book at the below address.

Larry is the founder and Artistic Director of the Belltown Theatre Center in Seattle, Washington. His address is: PO Box 16205, Seattle, WA, 98116. (206) 781-7305.

The
SANFORD MEISNER
Approach

The best-selling workbook that opens the door to Meisner's Approach

"Here, Silverberg, who was a student of the master teacher, presents a workbook for actors that will prove useful, regardless of how familiar the reader is with Meisner's methods. Silverberg's writing is concise and insightful throughout and makes the technique accessible to any committed student."
—*Library Journal*

"For serious theatre students, this book could be highly influential in laying a foundation for their acting careers."
—*Voice of Youth Advocates*

includes specific exercises from the Method
WORKBOOK ONE
ISBN 1-880399-77-6
176 pages, $12.95

Published by Smith and Kraus
available at your local bookstore
or call 1.800.895.4331

The Actor's Guide to Qualified Acting Coaches

VOLUME I: NEW YORK
VOLUME II: LOS ANGELES

Finding the right acting coaches to work with, those you can trust and learn from, those who are best suited for your own skill levels and career goals, can be an overwhelming undertaking. Now there's help!

The Actor's Guide to Qualified Acting Coaches *will lead you to the finest acting teachers in New York and Los Angeles through penetrating interviews with teachers and their students.*

New York Volume
ISBN 1-57525-009-8
160 pages $11.95

Los Angeles Volume
ISBN 1-57525-010-1
160 pages $11.95

Published by Smith and Kraus
at your local bookstore or
call 1.800.895.4331

Loving to
Audition
The Audition Workbook for Actors

**"A valuable, adventurous,
and enthusiastic entrée into the little defined
world of auditioning."**
Allan Miller, actor, director, teacher, and author

In *Loving to Audition*, Larry Silverberg's revolutionary book, you will learn the essentials and vital skills of great auditioning. You will learn how to bring your most passionate and creative self into the audition room, rather than leaving it outside the door! Most importantly, Larry guides you toward a shift in your experience of auditioning, from anxiety and fear to artistic pleasure, aliveness, and joy!

includes specific exercises
LOVING TO AUDITION
ISBN 1-57525-007-1
144 pages, $15.95

Published by Smith and Kraus
*available at your local bookstore
or call 1.800.895.4331*